The Life and Death of Juan Coy

The Life and Death of Juan Coy

Outlaw and Lawman

By
Charles L. Olmsted
and Edward Coy Ybarra

EAKIN PRESS Fort Worth, Texas

Copyright © 2001
By Charles L. Olmstead and Edward Coy Ybarra
Published in the United States of America
By Eakin Press
An Imprint of Wild Horse Media Group
P.O. Box 331779
Fort Worth, Texas 76163
1-888-982-8270
www.EakinPress.com
ALL RIGHTS RESERVED
1 2 3 4 5 6 7 8 9
ISBN-10: 1571683240
ISBN-13: 978-1571683243

ALL RIGHTS RESERVED. No part of this book may be reproduced in any form without written permission from the publisher, except for brief passages included in a review appearing in a newspaper or magazine.

Library of Congress Cataloging-in-Publication Data

Olmsted, Charles L.
   The Life and Death of Juan Coy : Outlaw and Lawman / by Charles L. Olmsted and Edward Coy Ybarra.
     p. cm.
   Includes bibliographical references (p.　) and index.
   ISBN 1-57168-324-0
   1. Coy, Juan Jose, 1842–1892. 2. Outlaws--Texas, South Biography. 3. Peace officers--Texas, South Biography 4. Frontier and pioneer life--Texas, South. 5. Coy family. 6. Texas, South Biography. 7. San Antonio Region (Tex.) Biography. 8. Nueces River Region (Tex.) Biography.   I. Ybarra, Edward Coy. II. Title.
F391.C785046   2000
976.4'35061'092--dc21
[B]   99-28428
                                                               CIP

Contents

Preface   v
Acknowledgments   vii
Introduction   ix

Chapter One/Early Days in South Texas   1
Chapter Two/War of the Rebellion and Reconstruction   6
Chapter Three/An Era of Dangerous Lawmen   21
Chapter Four/Five Years Without a Gun   33
Chapter Five/The Butlers and the Death of Helena   41
Chapter Six/A Little Less Work and a Lot More Trouble   58
Chapter Seven/Prejudice Amid Progress   68
Chapter Eight/Pursued by the Law   76
Chapter Nine/The Daileyville Riot   79
Chapter Ten/The Sensation of the Day   92
Chapter Eleven/Family Life   103
Chapter Twelve/A Tamer West   113
Chapter Thirteen/Visiting San Antonio   120
Chapter Fourteen/"Shoot me if you can . . ."   125
Chapter Fifteen/End of a Violent Era   139

Notes   149
Bibliography   163
Index   167

Preface

The research conducted in preparing this book has been not only informative and entertaining but also has precipitated several journeys. Traveling to some of the small towns south of San Antonio has given the authors greater appreciation of the area and of life in the cities and towns which are usually just names on signs along Interstate Highway 37.

Edward Coy Ybarra's lifelong love of Texas history was sparked at the early age of ten while on a road trip with his family. A highway sign marking the exit to Coy City triggered him to ask his mother the connection of the small Texas town to his middle name. She knew a familial connection existed with Coy City, but she was unable to add more detail.

In 1989, Edward Coy Ybarra finally began his quest for that connection. He methodically researched his family roots, and eventually uncovered the story of his great-grandfather Juan Coy.

Some towns, such as Indianola, were wiped out because of storms. Others died away for other reasons mostly unknown to us. Daileyville, which is the center of probably the biggest story in this book, is dead. Gone also are some of its neighboring cities: Couch, a black community; Cadillac, a Scandinavian town; and Lodi. There may be a family or two and a church still present, but that is about all. The reasons for their demise vary from economic to political to geographical.

Some towns are near death because there are no longer any businesses present, and families soon leave in search of work. Other old towns are dying quiet deaths because young families move to bigger cities, not just in search of jobs but also to be closer to better schools and more community activities. Some towns, such as Helena, were near death but are slowly being revitalized.

One habit we hope you will pick up is to occasionally take the backroads in your travels and stop to read the information on historical markers along the way. That sleepy old town you are passing through may have been jumping with excitement 100 years ago.

* * * *

Please note: The dialogue in this book is taken from newspaper articles, the diary of Jesse Perez, or other sources noted. Dialogue that is not footnoted in any way is conjecture on the authors' part, based on the events or mood at the time.

Acknowledgments

Most of the research for this book was conducted in libraries and courthouses. We wish to thank the library staffs from the City of San Antonio (microfilm and records sections), The Center for American History on the University of Texas campus, the City of Kenedy, the City of Runge, and Trinity University for their help. The district clerk's criminal divisions for Bexar County, Karnes County, and Wilson County were very helpful, not only in providing us information and helping decipher or translate 100-year-old documents but also in recalling stories which had been passed down. So, thank you very much, Rose Galvan of Bexar County and Patricia Brysch and Linda Kroll of Karnes County.

Brother Edward Loch, archivist for the San Antonio Catholic Archdiocese, and Chris Floerke of the Institute of Texan Cultures also provided much assistance.

Special thanks goes to Charlotte Nichols, who provided not only pictures, information and stories but did a lot of the early research on the subject. Appreciation also goes to Alex Coy, Arthur M. Coy, and Victoria Coy Ybarra for providing interesting historical notes. Much appreciation goes to Kelly Long for her editing expertise and valued support, as well as Dr. Laura Hendrickson, graduate adviser for communication arts at University of the Incarnate Word.

Deep appreciation goes to Col. E. A. Montemayor for his editing and insight into the culture of the period.

Thanks also to attorney Jay Brandon for his legal help and

Dennis Moreno and Norbert Martinez of Los Bexarenos for their genealogical advice.

A big thanks also goes to Ed Eakin, publisher, who liked what he saw from these two novice authors. Much appreciation is also extended to Melissa Locke Roberts, the book's editor.

Much of our thanks goes to our families, whose support and encouragement kept us going.

The credit for the book's success is shared by all those mentioned. The mistakes, if any, are ours in the end.

We hope you enjoy the book and learn how this history was shaped. When you're reading this book, parts of it may remind you of the adage that "The more things change, the more they stay the same." History can't be changed, and old habits are hard to change.

CHARLES L. OLMSTED
EDWARD COY YBARRA

Introduction

Killing was a way of life in the Wild West days of the 1800s, especially in Texas. The wide open range of uncivilized and unpopulated land seemed to breed killers. Indians, who had been pushed out from the East, terrorized underpopulated areas and tried to stay one step ahead of the U.S. Army and the Texas Rangers. The largest state in the country bordered Mexico, which was a safe haven and hideaway for many outlaws while producing many of its own. Life was a little better in populated areas, such as San Antonio and Austin, but the threat of gunfire was always present—anytime and anywhere.

The area around the Mexican border was particularly prone to gunfire. Laredo thrived as the gateway to Mexico and the last United States city on the biggest and busiest north-south passage into Mexico. The Rio Grande separates the two countries. An area just north of Laredo, known as the Nueces Strip, was a particularly cut-throat area. The Nueces Strip was so called because of the nearby Nueces River. No one was safe in the area. The area was almost barren and desolate, as it is even today. Cactus, brush, and mesquite trees provided little relief for humans and very little food for cattle. It was a perfect place for outlaws to hide out, though, and was even more dangerous in the 1800s. Robbers and killers lurked there because traders had to cross the area on the San Antonio-to-Mexico route.

Small towns that were in friendlier and more populated areas still had their share of problems. Everyone carried guns, and many an argument broke out in a saloon. Many towns made visitors "check their irons" at the city limits, but there always seemed to be a few who had an extra gun strategically placed. It was quicker and easier to settle an argument with a gun. People were quick to take sides in small towns, and aligning oneself with the wrong person could also be dangerous. The sheriff had the political power but didn't always have the economic power, which could include money, land, livestock, or water. Sometimes the political and economic leaders butted heads or, in many cases, it was law agency against law agency.

Of course, there were lawmen around to protect and defend the area, but sometimes they were as bad as the outlaws themselves. Many times, the lawmen were nothing more than outlaws with a badge. It was difficult at times to distinguish who was on which side. The gunfights weren't just outlaws against outlaws or lawmen against outlaws but could be lawmen against lawmen. Longevity was not a prevalent trait of the 1800s lawman. It was rare for a sheriff to live long enough to retire.

Shootouts involving lawmen and outlaws were not confined to the historic and Hollywood-glamorous O.K. Corral or Dodge City. They were regular occurrences in Texas. For whatever reason, be it the ethnicities involved (Mexicans and African-Americans) shooting among themselves or the less-than-glamorous characters, these shootings rarely caught the eye of the historians or Wild West writers.

One family always involved with the side of the law was the Coy family from South Texas. The most famous of the Coys was Juan Coy, who gunned down at least thirty-three men by his accounts.[1] Coy earned his hard reputation after the Civil War during the turbulent Reconstruction Period, and it followed him through his brushes with the law and his lifelong friendship with the Butler family from Karnes County.

But Juan Coy was not always wanted by the law. Most of the time he was a member of a law enforcement agency, having served as a deputy constable, a deputy sheriff and a deputy U.S. marshal. He also helped out Capt. Lee Hall of the Texas Rangers[2] and the justice of the peace in Von Ormy, Texas.[3] There are no official records of Coy being on the payroll as a deputy U.S. marshal, but officials say it was quite common back then to deputize people on the spot for a certain case and compensate them without any official documentation.

Juan's father, Antonio de los Santos Coy, was a "servant" for Capt. Jack Hays of the Texas Rangers.[4] Antonio was not on the payroll but served as scout and close confidant of Hays. Antonio traveled with Hays during battles against Mexican bandits and Indians, including the 1848 war against Mexico.

Two other Coys figure prominently in this story, which weaves its way through South Texas history from the Civil War into the 1890s. His cousins, Jacobo and Andres Coy, were law enforcement officers, and both did their share of killing with the badge. Both Coys were San Antonio city policemen during the 1880s. Another cousin, Pablino Coy, was a deputy sheriff who helped head off the Corpus Christi Raid by Mexican bandits in 1875.[5]

Jesse Perez, still another cousin of Juan Coy—actually a first cousin once removed—was also in law enforcement. Perez worked for the Texas Rangers, as a justice of the peace, and with the sheriff's office and a federal law agency. He was approximately twenty years younger than Juan Coy, but Perez recruited Coy to help him out on early law enforcement duties.[6]

As chronicled in *Journey Through Texas* by Frederick Law Olmsted, killing sometimes just happened, as when a stray bullet accidentally killed an innocent victim sitting in a restaurant near the Alamo.[7] (This happened in the 1850s, and still happens today as innocent people get caught in drive-by shootings.)

Juan Coy was the type of man one did not cross. Maxine Yeater Linder wrote in her autobiography titled "Wofford Crossing Road" that Coy "was one of the ugliest men living at the time, strongly resembling a lion. His disposition was even worse, and some claim that he used to go down into Mexico when there was trouble there just to be in on the killing."[8]

Despite his obvious shortcomings, though, Coy was loyal to his family and friends, and that loyalty was returned. Even those who hated him still respected his power. It was raw power, the type learned from hard living. Despite San Antonio and South Texas being predominantly Mexican-American, the Mexican-Americans were still treated as second-class citizens by the minority Anglo community (as it remains today in some cases).

When Juan Coy died on January 25, 1892, he was a deputy sheriff, from Floresville, who had been hired by Capt. Lee Hall of the Texas Rangers to guard a railway company's property during a strike.[9] It was the loyalty Coy showed to fellow workers which precipitated an argument.[10] It was loyalty to the Butler family which placed Coy in San Antonio protecting the railway company's property. Mr. Yoakum, the railroad owner, had received part of William G. Butler's land years before, along with money for the rights to build a rail line through his property.[11] Butler and Yoakum had become friends and business partners. Since Coy was a friend and employee of the Butler family, that also made him a friend of Yoakum's.

Coy always had the reputation and look of a dangerous rogue. The few photos and drawings of him show that he had a handlebar mustache and stubble on his chin, complemented by dark, menacing eyes. His sinister look more than compensated for his height of no more than 5'4½. He was stocky, though, weighing 175 pounds.[12] Coy earned his tough reputation as a youth in Atascosa County and continued to live up to it through the Civil War and later as a constable, deputy sheriff, deputy U.S. marshal, and hired gun for the Butler family.

Statehood did not improve civilization, as the Wild West lifestyle continued to exist for many years. Many a simple argument ended in gunfire. The guns were deadly but inaccurate. The bullets had a tendency to go astray and kill innocent bystanders, since most gunfights got their start with a liquor bottle nearby.

The average life expectancy for men in the late 1800s was the late thirties. Now in the mid-seventies, the increased life expectancy can be attributed to improved medical care and better sanitation. Both factors did make important contributions, but curtailing the use of guns as a bargaining tool in arguments also helped. Society was becoming more civilized, and more people were leaving the farm for the city and its industrial jobs.

The days of Jesse and Frank James, John Wesley Hardin, and others who made their living and built their reputation from the gun were dying. The Wild West Days were still alive in San Antonio, though. The Sporting District housed vaudeville theaters, houses of prostitution, saloons, and gambling halls—some offering all under the same roof. The clientele included Billy the Kid, Butch Cassidy, Kid Curry, and Sam Bass.[13] In 1882 alone there were 300 arrests for dealing monte, faro, bunco, keno, and other such gambling. There were also fifteen cases against women and one against a man for running houses of prostitution.[14] The area very seldom slept.

The country had pushed its boundaries from the Atlantic Ocean to the Pacific Ocean in less than 100 years, chasing the Indians to reservations or graves.

The times were indeed changing in the 1880s and 1890s, when Juan Coy made a name for himself in San Antonio and South Texas. Gunfights between law enforcement officers were still common, but that would change shortly after Coy's death. In his own way, the story of Juan Coy and his life and death reflected the life and death of the Wild West in South Texas.

CHAPTER ONE

Early Days in South Texas

The Coy family can trace their roots back to the early days of San Antonio and Texas. They are part of the military settlers and civilian Canary Islanders who established what later became San Antonio and Bexar County. Religious and cultural backgrounds show a heavy influence in the area's development. Many of today's small South Texas towns are still predominantly populated by the ethnicity that founded and settled them more than 100 years ago, such as the Germans in New Braunfels and the Poles in Panna Maria. In the 1800s most of these groups landed in Corpus Christi (Body of Christ) and made a three-day journey northwest to San Antonio. The area the Coy family settled most heavily is now Karnes, Atascosa and Wilson counties.

The first public schoolteacher in Texas was Don Cristobal de los Santos Coy, who started teaching in San Fernando de Bexar in 1746.[1] The first mission schools started in 1690 in East Texas at San Francisco de los Tejas. The school established by Santos Coy was the result of a joint agreement where the government donated the land, the church furnished the buildings, and the public maintained the area.[2]

The Coy family was one of the more influential and prosperous Mexican families in South Texas in the 1700s and 1800s. They were very generous with their time and resources in helping other families get settled, and that generosity was rewarded. Trinidad Coy, Juan's uncle and Ildefonso's father, was one of the early settlers of Karnes County.

When Juan's cousin Ildefonso Coy died in 1936, the *Kenedy Advance* recounted some of the Coy history[3] and revealed how the Coys helped out San Antonio families, regardless of race and risk to themselves.

One factor that led to the Battle of the Alamo was that the Americans surpassed the limit that Mexico had established for new settlers on their land. More and more Americans continued to move into Mexico-controlled Texas. Antonio López de Santa Anna, the Mexican general, declared it was enough. War broke out, and eventually the Texans won their independence at the Battle of San Jacinto. More families then moved into Texas in search of the tremendous farming and ranching opportunities.

The year 1840 saw Texas as a republic, a country on its own just four years after the victory for independence at San Jacinto but still five years away from joining the United States of America. The Wild West more than lived up to its name in Texas because of its republic status and the open range. Mexicans raided South Texas frequently, killing citizens and stealing cattle and horses. Mexico and West Texas were safe hideouts for outlaws from the Midwest. San Antonio was just a small town of 7,000 people, and south of there more sagebrush scattered through the dry, barren country than communities did.

In that era a band of Mexicans raided the ranch of John Twohig, a prominent Irish businessman and banker, chasing away cattle and horses.[4] The Mexican bandits fired off several rounds near the house to ward off any retaliation, but Twohig, his ranch hands, and friends were out in the fields at the time. Twohig and his group returned to the house, got their horses, and gave chase.

"Quick, get provisions and saddle up," Twohig instructed. "The Mexicans have done this too long and we need to fight back now. They have thirty minutes on us, but it is still two days to the border."

Twohig and his group were just a little too relentless in their pursuit across the 130-mile brush area; they soon found themselves in Mexico.

"John, that was the Rio Grande we crossed there," said one

man. "We're in Mexico . . . and you know what they do with Texans?"

"I know, plus we've lost them," Twohig said. "Let's turn back. We have to learn to defend ourselves better. We need some warning system when they cross the river and the plains."

"Too late, we've been spotted," another man noticed. "It looks like *federalistas*. Let's make a run. Too many to fight them."

The men quickly turned their horses around and spurred them in hopes of escaping the *federalistas*. The *federalistas* continued to give chase and were soon within firing range. A couple of shots over their heads quickly brought the men to a stop just south of the border and freedom. They didn't tell the *federalistas* they were chasing Mexican bandits because that would surely sign their death warrants.

The *federalistas* brought them to the nearest jail and kept them imprisoned there for more than a year. Word eventually crossed the Rio Grande and the desolate land to the San Antonio area about Twohig's plight. He and his men were scheduled to be executed when Trinidad Coy visited Mexico and intervened on the Texans' behalf. Coy talked to the officials, on a couple of occasions, while on trips into Mexico. His last visit was with money and extra horses as bribes to the officials. The Americans' lives were spared and they were released.[5] They had been prisoners for over a year, and their story circulated around San Antonio and South Texas. The incident gave the Texans a fight and resolve that had been missing, and resulted in a decreased number of border raids.

Grateful to Coy for saving his life, Twohig sent for him and gave him a job on his ranch along with half interest in the cattle and horses.[6] Years later Twohig gave "Coy and his wife and each of his children 40 acres of land—some 1,280 acres—for his interest in the stock."[7] Trinidad Coy's ranch was named Conquista, and it adjoined William Butler's spread near Kenedy.[8]

Twohig moved to San Antonio and got into the banking business. In June 1878 the *San Antonio Daily Herald* advertised "John Twohig—Commerce Street, Banker and Dealer in Foreign and Domestic Exchange, Coin and Bullion."[9] The June 11, 1878, issue of the *San Antonio Daily Herald* ran a short notice about a problem at Twohig's bank. Bank officials and skilled workmen toiled three days and nights before finally opening the large safe. The safe, which had resisted previous efforts, had to be broken into because someone had forgotten the combination.[10]

When Twohig died, he left his entire estate, including his ranch, to the Catholic church. The ranch covered an area from Karnes City to a few miles north of Falls City.[11]

The area just southeast of San Antonio was heavily populated by Polish immigrants. The oldest Polish Catholic church in America was established at Panna Maria. The Germans settled primarily forty miles north of San Antonio in New Braunfels, while the Poles stayed approximately fifty miles south of San Antonio. Geography may have placed them as neighbors in Europe, but that was their only similarity in Texas. The Poles wanted distance from the Germans, not wanting to be ruled by them.[12]

The Germans tried to control the Poles in culture and religion. The Germans were mostly Lutheran and skilled laborers, while the Poles—like the Mexicans—were Catholic and content with working the land. The Poles and Mexicans settled south of San Antonio, while the Germans were north of San Antonio. Hence, the Polish connection with the Mexicans.

The Silesian Poles and Mexicans were on friendly terms from the Poles' arrival. The Mexicans drove the Poles in ox-carts to their settlements after reaching Texas.[13] Mexicans and Silesian Poles soon became neighbors and many eventually became relatives. Young Poles learned their native tongue first, then Spanish, then English.[14]

Andres Coy, Sr., helped the Poles through the 1856-57 drought.[15] The area was without rain for fourteen months, which killed whatever vegetation was in the ground and stopped farmers from beginning any planting. The drought caused vegetable prices to skyrocket to $24 for 100 pounds of flour and $3 for a bushel of corn.[16]

Corn was not a popular crop in Poland, but the Poles quickly planted the main Texas crop upon their arrival. Andres Coy gave the Panna Maria settlers their first corn for bread and seed in late 1856.[17] The food item took on a different light for the Poles when one group showed them how tasty roasted corn ears were.

The Butler family was also helpful to the community when the drought hit in the summer or when the winter was especially cold.

William Green Butler came to South Texas from Mississippi in 1852 with his parents, Burnell and Sallie Butler.[18] Butler was eighteen years old when his family and their slaves reached the San Antonio River on Christmas Eve of 1852.[19] William G. Butler had eleven brothers and sisters. Burnell was deaf and mute from a childhood disease, and older brother Woodward died of yellow fever, which he contracted on a supply trip to Indianola in 1853. At the young age of twenty, Bill Butler was now spokesman and leader of the Butler family.[20] Burnell Butler would meet an untimely death in 1870 from falling off a cliff.[21]

The Butlers brought wealth and compassion with them. They befriended Mexican and Polish families during the early winters by providing them with food, cattle, and supplies to stave off the harsh elements and starvation.

"You have done enough, Mr. Butler," one Polish farmer told Butler. "We owe you our lives."

"Mr. Mocygozemba, you would do the same if we were in your shoes," Butler replied. "Take the firewood, corn, and venison. There is plenty to go around."

Some say that Butler's kindness had a price, though.

CHAPTER TWO

War of the Rebellion and Reconstruction

Texas was still a republic when Juan José Coy was born in 1842.¹ It was six years after the Battle of the Alamo and three years before Texas joined the United States as the twenty-eighth state. Juan Coy was born in a cabin on the Atascosa Creek near Pleasanton in Atascosa County.² He was born and raised on the wild frontier. No birth certificate or baptism record has been found. Coy's mother, Guadalupe Calderon,³ was believed to be a Lipan Apache, and Coy's father, Antonio, was a "servant" with Capt. Jack Hays' Texas Ranger group.

Juan's father, José Antonio de los Santos Coy, was born in 1799 in Rio Grande City and died from a stroke on January 18, 1891, in San Antonio.⁴ Antonio Coy married Guadalupe Calderon, but there are no records as far as a wedding date or how long the marriage lasted. Family stories, though, tell that Juan's mother was a Lipan Apache and that Juan's father left him to be raised by Trinidad, Antonio's younger brother.

Both Antonio and Guadalupe were part of Capt. Jack Hays' Texas Ranger squad. Antonio served as scout and was an unofficial member of the Rangers, even though he was regarded as a servant. Juan's mother was also a servant for the Rangers. Both came in handy as interpreters when the Rangers were fighting Mexicans or

Indians. The Lipans, a branch of the Apaches that claimed its territory from the Big Bend (near El Paso) to Laredo, joined the Rangers occasionally in fighting the Comanches. Traveling the frontier and going from battle to battle was no way to raise a child; hence the decision was made to leave Juan with Trinidad.

Antonio Coy "was not only captured but roughly treated for his known adherence to the Texan cause"[5] in repelling an 1842 attack by the Mexican army. Antonio Coy took Hays' livestock to San Francisco, California, while Hays, who was heading west for the Great Gold Rush, took a steamer to the West Coast in January 1850.[6] It is not known how long Coy stayed in California.

Trinidad, Antonio, and their three sisters—Juana Maria Luisa, Maria Antonia, and Maria Carmen—were born with the surname of de los Santos Coy, but it was this generation that opted to shorten the name to Coy.[7]

"I promise I'll raise him as if he were my own son," Trinidad told his brother before Antonio struck out for another battle. Antonio had just left his son, Juan, to be raised by his brother. "He is a part of this family just as you are. I understand your reason, but please remember he is still your son."

It is not known how much, if any, contact Juan Coy had with his father over the years.

Juan Coy was raised with Trinidad Coy's family and Alejos Perez' family. Trinidad Coy, who died in 1888, was married to Maria del Refugio Vara. They had eight children: José Manuel, born in 1848; Ildefonso, born in 1850; Trinidad, a daughter born in 1852; Antonio Paulino, born in 1854; Refugia; Emmet; Andres; and Jacobo.[8] The years of birth for the last four are unknown.

The Coys were among the earliest settlers of South Texas. Juan Coy was already a young boy when the Butler family, discussed in Chapter One, joined the masses moving into Texas.

Butler married Adeline Riggs Burris in January 1858 in Goliad County.[9] Adeline was born May 15, 1838, in Washington County, Ohio, to Benjamin and Susan (Riggs) Burris. They lived in Ohio and Galveston County, Texas, before settling in South Texas.[10] William and Adeline had two children before the Civil War broke out: Newton G., born December 7, 1858, and Helen Adeline, born April 22, 1860. A third, Louissa M., was born April 4, 1862, but it is not known if the elder Butler had already left for the war. He made at least one visit home during the war as Emmett W. was born November 8, 1864. Five children followed: Marion (born November 9, 1866), Sykes Charles (born in 1867), Cora Ann (born February 2, 1870), Theodore Green (born September 14, 1871), and William Green Butler, Jr., nicknamed "Hemis" (born November 8, 1876).[11]

The nation was inflamed with talk of slavery and the impending split of North and South. The political inaction to solve the slavery issue in the 1850s did nothing to quiet that talk, and with the 1860 election of Abraham Lincoln, the talk soon turned to action.

Karnes County followed the rest of the state and voted to secede from the Union. The legislature adopted a resolution on February 1, 1861, to leave the Union and join the Confederacy.[12] The War of the Rebellion, as it was called, finally broke out at Fort Sumter, South Carolina, on April 12, 1861. Texas was not solid in its support of the Confederacy. Sam Houston, former Republic of Texas president and U.S. senator, was deposed as governor because he did not want Texas to secede from the Union.

The Union had strong support in German communities, western settlements, and along the northern border areas. Some Union supporters quickly and quietly left the state while others turned to showing their colors for the Confederacy. Union sympathizers who were discovered faced hanging by vigilantes, home guards, or neighbors.[13]

The Singer family (of sewing machine fame) were Union sympathizers and were forced to abandon their ranch on Padre Island. Word circulated that they buried $80,000 in gold near the ranch headquarters and could not find it upon their return in 1867 because of hurricane damage.[14]

The issue in Texas was not so much slavery as it was states' rights. In the 1850 census, there were 7,747 slaveowners of the state's 154,034 white people. Each slaveowner had an average of seven slaves.[15]

William Green Butler volunteered for Confederate service and was mustered into the Escondido Rifles in July 1861[16] but did not report until 1862 as a private. His land was near Escondido Creek in what was Goliad (now Karnes) County. Butler commanded a company of mounted riflemen. He later joined Franklin C. Wilkes' cavalry and transferred to the Trans-Mississippi Department, which covered Louisiana, Texas, and Arkansas.[17]

Juan Coy was already hiding out around the country and found himself fighting for the North during the war. Coy, who wanted to be near the action, was listed as a bugler with a company of Texans who were in the Union Army.[18] More than 1,000 Anglo deserters from the Confederate Army and Mexicans who traveled to the Rio Grande area joined the Union forces. The Mexicans, despite living in the South, sympathized with the North. The South recognized the Spanish government's rule over Mexico. The North supported Mexico's autonomy. Most Mexicans from Texas joined the Union Army because of that allegiance.[19]

Juan Coy, who listed his occupation as stock raiser, joined H Company of the First Regiment of the Texas Cavalry (Union) on December 28, 1863, in Brownsville as bugler[20] at the age of twenty-two. Coy became a private in the fall of 1864 and was stationed at Brazos Santiago Island, Texas, with a special detachment for six months before being transferred to Company L in Baton Rouge, Louisiana, on March 14, 1865.[21]

Once the war commenced, Lincoln ordered a blockade of the Southern ports. The Union started battling in early 1862 over Brazos Santiago Island, the entrance to the Brownsville port, which shipped cotton. The North finally took control in November 1863, at which time they built a barracks for 950 men and had one warship anchored nearby.[22]

Confederate Col. John S. "Rip" Ford set up camp 165 miles away from Brownsville in 1864. Ford's men remained there even after Lee surrendered to Grant in April 1865. The 62nd U.S. Colored Infantry and the Second Texas Cavalry left Brazos Santiago on May 11 in search of Ford's men at Palmito Ranch.[23] The Confederates clearly won the last battle of a war which officially ended a month before. More than 100 Union men were killed while the South's toll was five wounded.[24] Coy was stationed at Brazos between the capture and the war's final battle.

Coy was mustered out October 31, 1865. He had been paid $220 bounty money and was still due $80 bounty money but owed $3.02 in his clothing account.[25] William G. Butler, in his early thirties at the time, met up with Juan Coy during the war. Butler realized that Coy could help him back home when the war was over.

| C | 1 Cav. | Texas. |

John Coy

Bugler, Co. C⚡, 1 Reg't Texas Cavalry.

Age ……… years.

Appears on
Company Muster Roll*
for Dec 28/63 to Feb 29, 1864.

Joined for duty and enrolled:

When………Dec 28……, 1863.
Where………Brownsville………
Period………3……years.

Mustered in:

When………Dec 28……, 1863
Where………Brownsville………
Present or absent………Present………

Stoppage, $………100 for………………………

Due Gov't, $………100 for………………………

Valuation of horse, $………100

Valuation of horse equipments, $………100

Remarks: *Appointed Bugler the 28th day of Dec 63*

* First current roll. No muster-in roll of this company on file.

Book mark: …………………………………

…………………………………… / ………………
(358d) Copyist.

John Coy's military records show him joining the Texas Cavalry in Brownsville in December 1863.

| 1 Cav. | Texas.

John Coy

Pvt., Co. H, 1 Reg't Texas Cavalry.

Appears on

Company Muster Roll

for Nov & Dec, 1864

Present or absent... Absent

Stoppage, $......100 for ......

Due Gov't, $......100 for ......

Valuation of horse, $......100

Valuation of horse equipments, $......100

Remarks: On detached service at Brazos St Iag. Texas by Sp. Ord. No 53. Hd Qrs. 1 Tex Cav Vol Morganzia La. Sep 9/64

Book mark: ......

(358) *Jnelly* Copyist.

John Coy's roll call for the Texas Cavalry indicates he was absent but on special orders.

| 1 Cav. | Texas.

Juan Coy

Pv't ......, Co. L, 1 Reg't Texas Cavalry.

Appears on

Company Muster Roll

for Mch & Apr, 1865.

Present or absent. Present

Stoppage, $ ____100 for ____

Due Gov't, $ ____100 for ____

Valuation of horse, $ ____100

Valuation of horse equipments, $ ____100

Remarks: 1st 2nd 3rd & 4th Installments of Recruit bounty due. Transferred from Co. K to Co. L by S.O. No. [illegible] Genl Carlos [illegible] & Remustered for three years from date of first enlistment by virtue of S.O. No. 37, Head Quarters, Northern Division of Louisiana March 9th 1865.

Book mark: ____

(858)   J. B. Taylor
                                          Copyist

Coy's record places him in Louisiana for part of the war.

Butler was taken prisoner, along with the entire command, at the Battle of Arkansas Post.[26] The prisoners from Arkansas Post were to be taken to Springfield, Illinois, by the Federals for imprisonment. The prisoners, upon their surrender, were ordered to stack their weapons, which they did. Tom Iles, Lieutenant Hitchcock, and Butler quietly walked away from the group during the confusion and escaped.[27]

Even after being away from the prison command, the three were on constant watch from the Federals because they were in the middle of the North's forces. They had to swim rivers and hide out as they slowly made their way south. They were hungry and tired but pressed on until they reached McCulloch's command. Once there, they were fed and sheltered and then ordered to join a refugee camp at Pine Bluff, Arkansas.[28]

One story has it that Butler learned during the war that thieves were taking his and his neighbor's cattle. He realized that the South was losing the war and it was a case of every man for himself. Butler escaped to return home to tend to his land and cattle.[29] Another version has it that after his escape and stay at the refugee camp, Butler joined Carter's command and finished the war in active duty in Arkansas and Missouri.[30]

Butler never saw the inside of a prison camp and was never wounded during the War of the Rebellion. He had just one furlough and otherwise endured all the hardships during his three years of service. He returned home with a strong military record.[31]

Butler started his business in 1862 with assets of $75,000 in land, $30,000 in buildings, and $100,000 in inventory.[32] He owned 10,000 head of cattle, 5,000 horses, 75,000 acres of land, and leased another 25,000 acres.[33] The business was financed from personal savings and bank loans from Frost National Bank in San Antonio and First City Bank in New York.[34]

A drought hit Karnes County and most of South Texas in 1863.[35] The creeks and rivers dried up and the lush grass soon withered away to a brittle, yellow nothing. Many cattle died soon after the grass withered away, but some cattle strayed over to the Nueces River, which kept them alive. Rains finally came in 1864 and ranchers went about rounding up their stray cattle. Some livestock had drifted as far away as San Diego in Duval County.[36] The cattle that wasn't recovered quickly by the rightful owners soon fell into the hands of opportunistic rustlers.

Upon returning home to Karnes County, Butler discovered that the word was true—much of their cattle and livestock had been stolen by rustlers. Taking advantage of the men who were away fighting the war, the rustlers rounded up cattle as they went along the countryside.[37] Trinidad Coy, Ildefonso's father and Juan's uncle, was too old for the war but stayed in Panna Maria as a member of the Panna Maria Grays. They served as the home guard during the Civil War but were greatly outnumbered by the rustlers[38] and were too old to mount any serious fight.

Butler and the other men rode north looking for their cattle and reached the band of rustlers near Bandera.[39] The thieves noticed Butler and his men approaching and stopped dead in their tracks. The leader of the rustlers rode out and met Butler, who also separated from his group.

"Be careful, Bill," one fellow rider whispered to Butler as he rode out to meet the rustler. "They've killed for less than this. We're behind you and ready all the way."

On both sides, men's hands were waiting by their side ready to draw on their guns. The cattlemen's chase that resulted in the showdown with the rustlers was bold but necessary. Some say such provocation was foolish, but the cattlemen stood up for their property. They had to show that they would not stand for such actions and that they would fight for their property. It was a principle that many a Texan had fought and died over.

Butler had gained a reputation as an honest and fair man since his move to South Texas. The head of the rustlers recognized Butler and rode out to meet him.[40] The two men with the biggest reputations in South Texas were face to face. The thief was evil and would shoot without any excuse. Butler was known as a courageous, unflinching man who was fair and just. This was during the days when a handshake sealed a deal and was better than a written contract. If Butler said it, that was good enough.

The two men eyed each other while both parties kept one eye on the center stage and the other eye on the group of men opposite them. The tension was thick with anticipation on both sides. Butler's group was scared. The thieves had never faced a showdown such as this. The slightest bit of hesitation on Butler's part or his men's part would spell the end to not only their bold stand but probably their lives.

The thief finally broke the silent tension. "What do you want, Mr. Butler?" he asked.

"To cut my cattle from that herd," Butler replied, never flinching from the statement which could have been his last.

"It is all right with me, sir," the thief said as he waved Butler through to the herd of cattle.[41] The other thieves looked bewildered but they knew they had been caught and should not risk lives in this type of stand. Besides, they still had other cattle in the herd to divide, and more could be stolen.

Butler waved his neighbors over to gather their cattle. The neighbors were a little hesitant and apprehensive at first, but they gained confidence once they realized that there would be no shooting. They kept their eyes on the thieves, though, in case greediness overcame common sense.

The two leaders stayed in the center as Butler's neighbors cut their cattle from the thieves' herd. Each side stared at the other in case violence erupted. There was none. All was peaceful.

"Thank you, sir, for your cooperation," Butler said after it was all over. "I'd appreciate it if your band of men stayed out of Karnes County on your raids."

"Mr. Butler, we've been hit hard up there. The war has left us without livestock, provisions, or farming equipment. The war has left many of us starving with little relief in sight."

"I know, but larceny of hard-earned goods is not the answer," Butler said with a tip of his hat as he brought the horse around and headed back south with his and his neighbors' cattle. Not one rifle shot was fired.

The Karnes County group hadn't traveled far when another band of men, led by Buck Pettus and Tom O'Connor, came riding up. Pettus told them they were tracking the same thieves and was amazed at how easily Butler handled the situation.[42]

"Mr. Butler, I realize this is a big request, but would you please accompany us back to the area where you found the band of men and help us in retrieving our cattle?" Pettus asked.

Butler was not the type of man to ignore a neighbor in need. These men were his friends, and Butler agreed to join them in visiting the thieves again. He sent his cattle back with the first group of men, along with instructions on where to take his cattle. He also instructed them to inform his wife, Adeline, of the situation and to tell her that the journey would take a little longer. Butler wound up negotiating the release of all cattle stolen from Karnes County and returned them to their owners.[43]

That courageous act was just another example of how Butler earned the county's respect and, ultimately, power. William G. Butler was a man who could get things done, rarely taking no for an answer. His power to accomplish things endeared him to the citizens of Karnes County, and with it came respect and loyalty.

He and the other men from Karnes County returned home from the Civil War in the spring and summer of 1865. Some companies didn't receive word of the South's surrender until May. The Union Army remained in the South to ensure peace and await the arrival of the Carpetbaggers and Reconstruction.

Coy was still single when war broke out. He was too busy being a cowboy, working ranches by day, and drinking and fighting by night. He left the army on November 4, 1865, in San Antonio.[44] He didn't have the promising future that Butler did. The lives of the two men from different backgrounds and lifestyles crossed many times throughout the years. Both yearned for various kinds of power and achieved it, many times in the same way.

The Trinidad Coy family had hundreds of acres in the Karnes City and Kenedy areas but sold it all to Butler shortly after the war. For the Coys, it was financial security. For Butler, it was the start of becoming a prosperous South Texas landowner.

South Texas in the summer is always hot and dry. Crops wilt under the heat. Livestock is always in danger of dying from the heat and lack of water. Many a creek or stock pond in March is transformed into a brown, cracked bed of earth crust by July. But the summer of 1865 was extra hard on everyone in the South. The war killed more than 50,000, left many men missing one or more limbs, killed off the wives and children the soldiers had left behind, and drove many people away from their homes. Unprotected livestock were killed and eaten during the war. Survival was the driving force. People ate whatever crops or animals were nearby, but nothing was replenished.

After four long years of fighting, the men returned home tired, underfed, ill, and wearing rags for clothes. Whatever family was still alive and present greeted them with open, loving arms, but the homecoming was short. The situation was just as bad at home.

War of the Rebellion and Reconstruction 17

There was more work to be done than they expected. Farmers were behind on planting crops. Livestock was scarce. Houses were in disrepair. The situation worsened as Carpetbaggers from the North moved in to steal even more power and resources from the South.

The Coys and Butlers retained their possessions and were not strongly affected by the Carpetbaggers. Neither immediate family lost any members to the Civil War. The Butlers continued to become leaders in South Texas. Other families flocked to them for assistance, and their power base expanded. The Coys sold a portion of their landholdings to the Butlers, which enabled the Coys to get through the Reconstruction period in the late 1860s.

Juan Coy was drinking in a bar one day in 1867 when some other cowboys started talking about the atrocities of the Civil War and Reconstruction. It was a discussion that wasn't uncommon around the South. One drunken man knew about Coy's past and told the maddening crowd, "This traitor fought for the Yankees. He killed some of our friends and relatives. He sold us out."

Coy just looked at the bottom of his glass. The drunk continued to harass and taunt Coy. Some customers circled around the drunk as he inched closer to Coy. The man carefully shifted his beer mug to his left hand. Coy noticed this and slowly raised his left bushy eyebrow.

The drunk moved a little closer, but Coy still had not moved. Some of the other drinkers also moved closer. Coy glanced at all of them, but not one was even close to reaching for his gun. The drunk drew his finger up to stick it in Coy's face. Coy seemed to leap up as if a gazelle and threw his right fist into his opponent's face. The man fell back and hit his head on the bar's edge and quietly slumped down. A couple of the man's friends rushed Coy and pinned him against the bar. The drunk slowly raised up and slammed his fist into Coy's stomach twice. The three took turns punching Coy in the stomach and face. The rest of the crowed cheered on the attackers and started chanting "Dixie . . . Dixie."

Coy's face was bloody by the time the third man started wailing on him. Coy curled up his legs, and just when the third man was moving in to punch Coy he thrust his right leg into the man's groin, sending him into a slow-bending crouch. The other two men moved to their friend's aid, and that was all the opportunity Coy needed. First, he took a bottle from the bar and smashed it over one man's head. Coy was just getting ready to look for the other man when the breath went out of him. His neck, shoulder, and chest suddenly grew cold and wet. The inside of him started burning, though. He turned around slowly to see a hand raising out of his back which was dripping blood. Coy squinted a bit more and noticed that the man was holding a six-inch knife. Slumping to the floor, Coy slipped into semiconsciousness. The three men each spat upon Coy and walked out of the bar.

The bartender rushed around to the front and picked up Coy's near-lifeless body. He grabbed a towel off the bar and quickly applied it to the back. Coy had been stabbed in the neck, and the knife had gone down and slightly to the right but not enough to where it penetrated the right lung.[45]

The wound slowly healed, but as a result Coy developed rheumatism in the last four years of his life.[46]

Most of the Coys drifted into law enforcement work. Juan Coy did, too, but seemed to drift back and forth over the line between law enforcer and law breaker. Most of the Coy family worked off and on for the Butlers throughout the years, and the Coys were called upon by the Butlers for special assignments, such as Juan guarding the railroad. A special relationship developed between the members of the two families, but the employer-employee formality remained.

Butler began driving cattle north to such places as Amarillo, Texas, and Kansas and Nebraska in March 1868. When he finished almost twenty years later, it was estimated he drove more than 100,000 cattle up north. The end to Butler's cattle driving wasn't the end to his cattle days, though; it just signaled a new direction. Transporting cattle became faster and cheaper as trains became more prominent[47] and barbed wire fenced off lands. Bill Butler, referred to as Colonel although he never reached that rank during the war, was in charge of the early cattle drives. Those drives ranged from one to three a year, but he had plenty of help from his brothers Robert and Wash Butler and ranch hands such as John Sullivan, Jim Nelson, John Brady, Juan Mendez, and Levi and Bill Perryman. Butler's other brothers, Pleas and Fayette Butler, led later drives along with Bud Jourdan and Ildefonso Coy.[48]

The Butler family started gathering and buying land as soon as they arrived in Texas from Mississippi. At the height of his power,

Butler owned more than 75,000 acres of land in Karnes County and leased another 25,000 acres. He had 10,000 head of cattle roaming some land and farms on the rest. Butler was a cattle drive partner with Seth Mabry, who had been a Confederate major in the Civil War. Mabry's domain was in Mason and Kimble counties. He had one of the most gorgeous houses in Austin in the 1870s and entertained guests there frequently.[49]

Butler's ranch was not the largest ranch in South Texas. The King Ranch, further south in the Valley, contained 1,200,000 acres. The XIT, which was in the Panhandle, was 3,050,000 acres when it was established in 1885. The ranch, spreading over ten counties, was given by the State of Texas in exchange for funds to build the State Capitol.[50]

Butler's power started eroding in the 1880s as different people filed suits against him for improper land acquisition.[51] Many of the suits he staved off, and the Butler family continues to this day to own a good portion of land in Karnes County. The family retains a prominent position in South Texas.

Butler was rich with land and, consequently, power. The Butlers and Coys survived Reconstruction. Bill Butler had almost a feudal type of system in Karnes County, but he did not abuse the power. He was very humane, and it was rare for anyone to have an unkind word about him during the 1860s and 1870s, at least publicly. The Coys were just some who prospered thanks to Butler.

Butler was a modest man. Years after his death, part of his land helped form a town in western Karnes County. Instead of naming it for himself, Butler left instructions for the town to be named Coy City after the Ildefonso Coy family. It was called Appleville for a time and reached its peak in the late 1940s, with 150 residents and five businesses.

Two of the buildings in the sparsely populated Coy City, which is named for the Coy family.

CHAPTER THREE

An Era of Dangerous Lawmen

Jacobo Coy was similar to his cousin Juan in several ways. Jacobo was also known to be on both sides of the law, although he tipped toward law enforcement much more than Juan did. Most of the Coys enjoyed their liquor, but Juan was the worst. He was mean enough sober and got into his share of fights, but when he was drunk, even his family feared and avoided him. Another cousin, Jesse Perez, said that Juan Coy would rather fight than eat.

Jacobo Coy found himself playing major roles in two of San Antonio's more infamous murders of the 1880s—both involving Ben Thompson at the Crystal Palace. Both are cases where it was impossible to know which side of the law the lawmen were on.

The first murder occurred July 11, 1882. Jack Harris was one of three owners of the Crystal Palace, a dance hall, theater, and saloon with some gambling on the side.[1] Ben Thompson lost a large sum of money that evening in cards at the Crystal Palace. He accused Joe Foster of running crooked card games.

Foster just sneered at Thompson and said, "That's just a cheap try at welshing on your bet."

Harris, hearing the accusation and sensing a fight, arose to defend his employee. Thompson saw Harris make a quick move toward him, felt threatened, and reached for his revolver. One shot rang out as Thompson fired, hitting Harris in the right lung.[2] Harris died almost instantly.

Thompson calmly walked out of the Crystal Palace and surrendered his six-shooter to Jacobo Coy, who was a city detective at the time but also a private policeman or bouncer at the Crystal Palace. Billy Simms, one of Harris' partners, rushed out pointing his finger at Thompson and shouted: "That dirty dog killed Jack Harris. It was plain murder."[3]

Harris was one of the more popular men in San Antonio. He knew all of the important visitors to the Crystal Palace and was a jovial, personable owner. He knew most of the local politicos and policemen, since both were frequent customers.

Thompson was an Austin marshal who had already shot and killed twenty Anglo men and countless Chinese, Mexicans, Indians, and African Americans.[4] The crowd outside took on a lynch mob attitude and wanted to hang Thompson right there on the spot, which was not uncommon in those days.[5]

Coy stood his ground, shaking his revolver at those chanting "Let's hang him," and marched Thompson off to jail.

The shouts grew even louder when Thompson was acquitted in the 22nd Judicial District Court of Judge George Noonan,[6] who later represented San Antonio in the U.S. Congress as a Republican. Again, San Antonio police officers protected Thompson as he was driven to the railroad station just blocks west of the courthouse. Fall was closing in but the heat was still oppressive, which made the vocal crowd even more hostile.

Thompson's reception at the Austin railway depot was totally different from his San Antonio sendoff. The crowd was cheering wildly, waving, and shooting pistols while a band played in the background.[7]

Thompson left San Antonio a free but bitter man. The Austin homecoming celebration picked up his spirits, and he enjoyed walking through the throng of well-wishers, shaking hands with old friends and relishing a hero's welcome. Thompson was indeed something of a hero as he and his wife, Mary Anne, despite having three children of their own, had also been foster parents to many children through the ages.[8]

Despite the legal victory, something still gnawed at Thompson. It wasn't the shooting, the court battle, or the rude reception from San Antonio. It was the card cheating by Joe Foster that set the whole ugly incident in motion.[9]

"Joe Foster is a crook, plain and simple," Thompson declared. "Joe is a card cheat and doesn't mind if he ruins people."

Thompson wanted revenge on Foster and told many friends around Austin about his intentions. Word eventually got back to San Antonio and the police department, including the arresting officer Jacobo Coy, about Thompson being hell bent and determined to gain revenge.[10]

The entire San Antonio police force knew Thompson, so there was no need for a description or an explanation of the situation. The unofficial word from San Antonio was for Thompson to stay out of town lest there be retaliation for killing Jack Harris.

Thompson didn't like the snub. He was an officer of the law and he could go anywhere he pleased in that capacity. The order—even though unofficial—grated on him. He was stubborn and mad enough about it to ignore it but not brave enough to rush out and flaunt it. Being a lawman didn't prevent him from being a target.

It was almost two years later before Thompson finally built up enough courage to make a trip to San Antonio. The day was March 11, 1884.

Joe Foster's snide remarks and the card cheating still festered in Thompson's craw. Thompson came across a new but trusted and good friend that fateful March day in King Fisher, the acting sheriff from Uvalde.[11] Fisher had fifteen fatal shootings to his credit as a lawman. He had a reputation as one of the most deadly shots in the Southwest.[12] The two lawmen started drinking and reminiscing about the old days, women, and the criminals they'd caught and shot.

"King, you've got to see the show 'Lady Audley's Secret,'" Thompson told Fisher during one of many stops in an Austin saloon. "The show is great and you will be smitten with the show's star, Ada Gray. You must see her. I saw last night's show, and she is more than beautiful."

A couple of other patrons echoed Thompson's sentiments and were rewarded with a shot of whiskey from Thompson's bottle.

"Okay, my curiosity is piqued," Fisher declared. "Let's go see this wonder woman, Ada Gray. Which theater is she at?"

"The show left town early this morning," one fellow drinker said. Thompson and Fisher both looked disappointed.

"Where is she now?" Fisher asked.

"The Turner Hall Opera House in San Antonio," he said rather matter-of-factly.

Thompson didn't look too well now. Fisher knew the story about the Harris shooting and trial. He also knew that his good friend was not welcomed in San Antonio and hadn't been back there in two years. He was not going to press the issue.

"Hell, we'll just go see the show," Thompson declared. "Ada Gray is worth the trip."

"Ben, are you sure you want to go to San Antonio?" King reasoned. "I don't want to get you in trouble. The show will be back around. Hell, it'll probably be in Uvalde soon, too."

"No, I can't be pushed out of a town like that. I was exonerated by their jury and court system, and I want to go." Thompson looked at his friend with cold, steely eyes. Fisher knew there was no talking him down from this challenge. "We're going to San Antonio to see Ada Gray. Another round, keeper."

That shot of whiskey was a little harder on Fisher than the previous ones. They were going to San Antonio. If Thompson wasn't worried, why should he be? After all, he thought, he wasn't the one who had been unofficially ordered to stay out of San Antonio.

The two lawmen left the saloon, unhitched their horses, and made their way to the railway station. They left the horses in a nearby livery with instructions that they would return tomorrow because they wouldn't be in any condition to return to Austin after the show.

The train carrying Thompson and Fisher had barely pulled out of the Austin station when word was telegraphed to the San Antonio police that Thompson was on his way: "Ben Thompson and King Fisher en route to San Antonio. Have been drinking and may make trouble."[13] Fisher was not welcomed in town either, since he was accompanying Thompson. The whiskey didn't increase their welcome.

Word was already on the streets among the San Antonio policemen that Thompson was on his way. Men were dispatched immediately to the Crystal Palace—inside and outside. The saloon's management, especially Joe Foster, was notified of the visitors. The telegram said nothing about Thompson's and Fisher's intention, but it was a sure bet that Thompson would make a call on the Crystal Palace and Joe Foster.

Men were already posted at the railroad station. Sharpshooters were posted at the railway station, the Crystal Palace, and other key points. The police even swore in ten sharpshooters as special officers to bolster their force.[14] The orders were simple: the two visitors were to be followed everywhere they went. The plan was to divert them away from the popular area to across the creek or red light district, which was also known as the Sporting District. Brothels were on every corner there, and fights were always breaking out. Gunfire wouldn't be that much of a surprise in this area. It was a nice arrangement between the police and the brothels. The police kept the area clean and didn't bother the women, and the women kept to their own little area. Everyone knew the boundaries. In fact, the police acted as tourist guides for visiting men who requested company.

Thompson and Fisher headed straight for the Turner Hall Opera House upon their arrival. The drinking continued on the train, as is evidenced by the swagger from both men. As manager of the Opera House, Tom Howard had put up with men like this only too often.[15]

"I'm Ben Thompson, marshal from Austin, and I brought my friend, King Fisher, sheriff from Uvalde, over here to see Ada Gray," Thompson slurred. "I've been telling him about her wonderful performance in 'Lady Audley's Secret' and he just has to meet her."

"I'm sorry, gentlemen, but Miss Gray is busy dressing now in preparation for the show," Howard said. "You can have a seat in the bar and wait for the show to begin."

"C'mon, Ben, let's have a seat," Fisher urged. "Maybe we should get something to eat before we drink some more. I could go for a juicy steak."

"Naw, we'll wait right here and bring us a bottle," Thompson demanded. "Tell Miss Gray her friend Ben Thompson is here. She'll see us."

"I'll see what I can do," Howard said, rolling his eyes as he ushered the two lawmen to the bar. He then took a quick leave for the backstage area. A city policeman was standing by the theater door and motioned for Howard to join him. This was great, Howard thought—all of these law enforcement officials, and they're all intoxicated.

"What do those two men want?"

"They want to meet Ada Gray, the star of the show, but they are way too drunk," Howard said.

"Both are dangerous men. Don't give them any reason to get mad, but don't let them become too forceful," warned the policeman. "There are a couple of officers in here, so you have nothing to worry about. We're trying to quietly run them out of town and back to Austin, but we will take action if necessary."

"Thanks . . . I must attend to my show now," said Howard as he hurried off backstage.

Everything was normal except for the occasional loud laugh and clinking of glasses from the Thompson-Fisher table. The piano playing signaled the seating for the show. Thompson and Fisher headed for the theater with their whiskey bottle in hand. It was common for bottles and drinks to be brought into the theater area. Thompson and Fisher were the only two in the crowd, though, who started drinking so early. It showed as they stumbled around trying to find seats and displayed obnoxious behavior. They swaggered toward the dressing area once more, only to find Howard blocking their path.

"Did you give Ada our last message?" asked Thompson. "She still hasn't come out to see us. Tell her Ben Thompson is here and we want to see her."

"I'm sorry, gentlemen, but she is busy getting ready for the show," Howard replied. "I'm sure as soon as the show is over, she'll be glad to talk with you."

Thompson and Fisher tried to slide past him, but Howard stood firm and the two did not pass. Dejected, they turned back and returned to their seats. A policeman in a nearby corner nodded at Howard.

The show started and everything went smoothly. Thompson nudged Fisher a couple of times to point out Ada Gray and how beautiful she was. They continued drinking.

"What in the hell is she singing about, Ben?" Fisher asked his friend. "I can't understand a thing."

"I don't know, King, but she sure is pretty," Thompson smiled. "Who cares what she's singing."

Thompson and Fisher tried once more to see Ada Gray but with no luck. They finally left, and Howard was able to breathe a sigh of relief. Howard watched them leave and noticed that the policeman and three others followed a short distance behind.

Thompson and Fisher headed for the bridge to the Sporting District. The policemen were thrilled that the plan to draw them away from the general population was working. Unfortunately, the two men made a detour. They stopped in at Gallagher's Saloon for another whiskey. A card game was going on, and Thompson eyed it with interest.

"Joe Foster," Thompson muttered. Fisher winced at the name.

Thompson and Fisher staggered across the St. Mary's Street bridge and finally up to the Crystal Palace. Thompson hadn't been there since that fateful day in 1882. Out in front, just as the last time he was there, stood Billy Simms smoking a cigar.[16]

"I'll be damned," Simms muttered under his breath. He waved at both of them and ushered them inside. Thompson and Fisher stood at the bar and looked at John Dyer, who had been tending bar the night Jack Harris was slain.[17]

"What'll it be, gents?" Dyer asked the two newcomers.

Both Thompson and Fisher answered in unison, "Whiskey."

The lawmen and Simms exchanged small talk for a minute. Simms tried to get Thompson and Fisher to cross the creek to the Sporting District. Simms looked as if he had been shot when Thompson answered, "No, Billy, we've decided to watch the show from the balcony."

Upstairs was Joe Foster, the man Thompson swore he would kill.

Simms was shaken by Thompson's last sentence, but the two visitors never noticed because they were so drunk. Simms, ever the gracious host, politely escorted them upstairs but to the opposite side of the balcony from where Foster sat for the vaudeville show. The two weren't in their seats too long before Thompson got restless again and arose, only to find Simms right behind him. Simms was nervously watching all three men, trying to keep the lawmen away from Foster. Simms soon ran out of luck.

"Billy, I'm going to take your suggestion," Thompson said. "Let's make that run across the creek."

Fisher looked happy that they were finally on the verge of winding down this night's escapades and hooking up with some women instead of all the shadow chasing.

Simms was behind the two men, showing them back down the stairs and hopefully out the door. Despite the handful of policemen stationed around the Crystal Palace, Simms still felt vulnerable. He was thinking that he was just a minute or two away from averting a disaster, but then it happened.

Thompson stopped cold at the stairs and whirled around. It caught Fisher and Simms off guard.

"I've got to see Joe Foster before we go," Thompson said.

"Ben, are you crazy?" Simms trembled. "Joe doesn't want to talk to ya or see ya. Stay away from him. Let's get out without any trouble."

"To hell with that talk," Thompson said. The whiskey caused him to stagger as he headed to a table. "I want to shake hands with Joe. That's all. No hard feelings."

The three men were soon joined by a fourth at the table. City policeman Jacobo Coy stepped out of the shadows on the balcony and placed himself close to Thompson, who realized the presence of a new person. Thompson slowly turned around and glanced at Coy. He did a double take, as Coy was the officer who arrested him after shooting Jack Harris less than two years before at the Crystal Palace. Thompson respected Coy because he had been doing his job and he also had protected him from an angry crowd. It was the same thing Thompson would have done to a prisoner if it occurred in Austin. But now he was being tracked down like an animal, and he let Coy know his feelings.

"You can go some other place, officer. I've been behaving myself," Thompson pleaded. "What's the matter, you don't trust me? How many more around here to keep track of me? Or am I a marked man?"

"Just making sure everyone stays alive while you're in San Antonio," Coy responded coolly. "Including you."

"I appreciate your concern, but my friend and I are fine and quite capable of protecting ourselves," Thompson said.

All the time, Thompson scanned the crowd on the balcony. Just then Thompson spotted Foster and called to him: "Hey, Joe, let's shake hands. Come on over."

Foster had been spotted and there was no honorable way for him to retreat from the scene without losing face. He moved slowly toward Thompson while others on the balcony recognized both men, remembered the situation from two years before and the stories since, and proceeded to back away from the center of the action. Policemen and constables were sent upstairs to try to keep the peace. Among the policemen was Andres Coy. All were making slight movements with their right hands toward their hips, double checking to see if their pistols were strapped.

The vaudeville show was downstairs, but the action on the gas-lit balcony was the center of attention that night with Thompson, Fisher, and Foster playing major roles. Foster slowly approached as Simms backed away. Thompson held out his right hand and smiled at Foster. "Joe, I just want to shake hands with you."

Foster looked Thompson square in the eyes with a dangerous look. "Ben, I've told you there's room enough in the world for the two of us, but I will never shake hands with you."

All eyes were on the pair in the center of the balcony. The tense silence was as thick as the smoke hanging in the Crystal Palace. After a few seconds, Thompson broke the silence: "Well, come take a drink with me."

"No," came Foster's stern reply, soon to be his last.[18]

Thompson whipped out his pistol. "Well, take this then." He struck Foster in the mouth with the pistol butt. At the same time, Jacobo Coy grabbed the pistol's barrel as Thompson pulled the trigger. The barrel and the close shot hit Foster in the face, knocking him to the ground.[19]

Coy pulled out his own pistol and shot at Thompson. Fisher joined in the struggle, and Coy lurched the pistol toward the other lawman. Coy was late with breaking up the fight as Foster hit the ground instantly. Coy instinctively pulled off a couple of shots from close range at Thompson, also ending his life instantly. Shots came from the curtained stalls where other San Antonio police officers were stationed. King Fisher, riddled with bullets, died before he even had a chance to draw his gun.

The patrons upstairs fell on the floor and hid under tables or behind corners as the first shot was fired. The show downstairs stopped and those customers strained to see who was involved in the shooting, but tried to remain hidden.

The shooting lasted less than thirty seconds. The clouds of smoke from the balcony and the stalls hung over the room. Fisher, Thompson, and Foster were all killed instantly, lying crumpled together on the floor.[20] Fisher had one arm across Thompson's body as if trying to protect his friend even in death.[21]

Another story reported that Foster survived the shooting but lost a great amount of blood and had to have his left leg amputated above the knee. Foster died later at Jack Harris' old house.[22]

Foster and Thompson despised each other. The shooting started that night because Foster wouldn't shake hands or have a drink with Thompson. Considering Thompson's state of mind and alcohol content, it's doubtful Foster would have survived the evening even if he had been a perfect gentleman. Thompson wanted revenge at any cost.

Thompson and Fisher both had hair-trigger tempers which could unleash at any second, resulting in shots being fired. One story about that fateful night had all four leading characters seated together at a table. That story is doubtful, considering all of the shooting and movement. Since Fisher's two guns were still holstered, it's possible that he may have been seated while the others were standing.

By the time the shooting was over and the coroner had done his work, seventeen bullet holes were counted in Thompson's body, including two in his heart. Fisher had been felled by twelve shots. Jacobo Coy, who was slightly injured in the shooting, was the only person ever mentioned as a shooter in the incident. The other gunmen who downed Thompson and Fisher were never named, but it was alleged that they used deer rifles. No one was ever indicted for the killings.[23]

One story had it that the bartender was the main culprit and that he used a double-barreled shotgun loaded with buckshot.[24]

Fisher was thirty and Thompson forty-two when they died. They had lived short but wild lives. Thompson had given Fisher a picture of himself earlier that day, and it was still on Fisher when he was killed.[25]

San Antonio residents cheered the news of the end of Ben Thompson and King Fisher, two lawmen who worked the wrong side of the law more than the right side. The *San Antonio Evening Express*' headline blared: "A Good Night's Work."[26]

Jacobo Coy was looked upon as a hero by killing the two outlaws. Mexican officers had always been considered second-rate by citizens, but the shooting gained popularity for Coy and helped along the acceptance of the few other Mexican officers. Jacobo Coy was a humble man and grudgingly accepted all of the praise.

While the San Antonio residents showered praise on Coy, citizens from Austin and Uvalde threatened to kill him. The city police had special details at the train station for a period after the killing just to ensure that no gunmen rode in from Austin or Uvalde in search of Coy.

Residents of Austin and Uvalde, where the two lawmen resided and were regarded as heroes, claimed the killings were an ambush and angrily protested the murders. Complaints were many, but retaliation was zero.

Thompson had been elected city marshal of Austin in December 1880. He was on the wrong side of the law most of his life, beginning as a thirteen-year-old when he was on trial for shooting a friend. He didn't spend any time in jail for that murder.[27] He was in New Orleans when he was eighteen and killed a Frenchman in a knife fight. He skipped town with the help of friends who brought him back to Austin.[28]

Thompson was constantly in trouble. After the Civil War, he fought in Maximilian's war in Mexico. He returned to Austin, was convicted of attempted murder of his wife's brother, and served two years. After prison, he went to Kansas for his favorite hobby—gambling. Thompson owned the Bull's Head Saloon in Abilene, Kansas, and then later was the house dealer at the Long Branch Saloon in Dodge City, Kansas. Eventually, he returned to Austin and bought into the Iron Front Saloon. There he stayed busy with two other hobbies—drinking and shooting. He beat another murder charge in 1876 and tried to improve his status by running for city marshal. He lost the first election but won the second.[29]

Honor among thieves certainly applied here, and Austin became a quiet city as criminals left town or reformed, not wanting to tangle with someone worse than themselves. Thompson tried his best to quell his drinking and set a good example of a law-abiding citizen. For the most part, he succeeded in Austin— but he traveled to San Antonio to enjoy himself. He had been in his last trouble just six years earlier, and he was already back in trouble with the killing of Jack Harris.

King Fisher once boasted that he had killed thirty-seven men, "not counting Mexicans."[30] Fisher started his criminal career at age fifteen when he stole a horse. The owner didn't press charges, but Fisher was later sent to prison for breaking into a house and was pardoned four months later.³¹ Fisher bought a ranch on Pendencia Creek and built a kingdom from southwest of San Antonio to the Mexican border. He ruled the lawless area from Castroville to Eagle Pass, which was a haven for rustlers, drifters, and criminals. There was a sign in the area which read: "This is King Fisher's road. Take the other."³² The land had plenty of brush and mesquite trees, too small to hang someone. Fisher and his men improvised by tying a person's neck to a tree and his feet to the saddle of a fast horse. They rode the horse until the head was ripped off the body.

Fisher ruled the area with his band of 100 men, stealing livestock and other property in broad daylight. No one would bother stopping them because the result would be death.³³

King Fisher and nine of his men were captured June 4, 1876, in Nueces by Capt. L. H. McNelly of the Texas Rangers. The men were taken to Eagle Pass but were released despite the opinion that seven of them could easily have been convicted of murder. McNelly rounded up 800 head of cattle, but they were also turned loose when no one came forward to claim the cattle. The thieves kept the cattle in Nueces, where no citizens would dare utter a word about the stolen property. The cattle would then be driven to market in Kansas. Some reported that the Nueces citizens, silent partners in the thievery, said Fisher's band of thieves were much worse than Indians when they were on the warpath.³⁴

One man and his two sons had gone to a corral to ask for the return of their cattle. They were shot dead before they could even finish hitching their horses.³⁵

Fisher and his gang of men would ship the stolen cattle up to Abilene and on to Kansas City. The Civil War had just ended, but Texans such as Shanghai Pierce and Fisher were dealing with the Yankees like long lost friends. The fact that Fisher was an outlaw and killed regular townspeople made him many enemies, but to be in business with the Yankees made it even worse.³⁶

Fisher toned down his criminal ways after the run-in with McNelly. He married in April 1876 and bought a ranch near Eagle Pass. He became a deputy sheriff in Uvalde in 1881 and acting sheriff two years later, when the sheriff was indicted.³⁷ He became an efficient and popular sheriff and was planning to run for office in 1884 when he made the fateful trip to San Antonio with Ben Thompson.

CHAPTER FOUR

Five Years Without a Gun

Juan Coy worked as a cowboy for William Butler, riding on some of the long cattle drives north to Amarillo, Dodge City, and Abilene. He helped out around the ranch, branding cattle and hauling bales of hay to the pasture. Coy was also Butler's hired gun and helped protect the Honey Ranch from Mexican raids from the south and Indian raids from the west. The Nueces Strip was notorious as a headquarters for Mexican bandits and blood-thirsty Americans who would raid Texas ranches and steal cattle and horses.

One of the worst Mexican bandits was Juan Nepomuceno "Cheno" Cortina, who was based near Brownsville. Cortina was a Robin Hood type who stole from Anglos and gave to his fellow Mexicans. He ruled the border in the 1860s and 1870s, and his men were responsible for at least 250 deaths.[1] Cortina was blood-thirsty and hated Anglos. The reason for his hatred of Anglos was obvious; his family had once owned a large amount of Texas real estate from a Spanish grant.[2] He thought "Mexico had been rooked out of the Nueces Strip as well as individual parcels of land within it."[3]

Cortina was also a businessman. He and his band of rustlers stole livestock and shipped it to Cuba under contract. His power and business were on both sides of the Rio Grande, as he also directed his empire from Matamoros, Mexico.[4] He ruled from the

Rio Grande north to the Nueces Strip, where King Fisher would later take over.

Juan Coy and Butler's other ranch hands were able to thwart any serious attack from raids by the likes of Cortina on Butler's ranch.

When Coy wasn't working with the cattle or keeping the ranch safe, he rode to Floresville to work as a deputy sheriff. Sheriff Ximenes and Coy had been friends for years, and Coy always lent a hand when Ximenes called. Ximenes had other regular deputies, but when he was tracking or going to arrest one of the tough fighters or lawless gunmen, he always tried to find Coy. Ximenes knew Coy was cut from the same cloth, and who better to track and capture a fierce gunman than another one? Coy helped collar quite a few criminals, which helped the family finances.

Being a deputy sheriff had other advantages, such as allowing him to be a little above the law when it came to drinking, fighting, and gambling. He tried to watch his behavior when he was in Wilson County. Not only did he try to obey the law because of his deputy sheriff status, but this was also where he was a husband and father.

Jesse Perez, Coy's cousin, wrote a journal about his law enforcement days. Perez' diary provided more information, although it is not known how reliable or accurate it was. It did, however, offer a closer glimpse of Juan Coy than newspaper articles provided. Perez' writing and grammar in the diary are difficult to understand. The feeling for the times and the people is very much alive, though. This remains the only other documentation of Coy's exploits besides newspaper articles. Perez was a relative and confidant of Coy's. He was a witness to not only Coy's actions but his thoughts as well.

Perez' diary states that the case which sent Coy to prison started in 1881.[5] (There is conflicting information due to contradictory documentation from the Texas Department of Criminal Justice and the *San Antonio Daily Herald* stories. Whatever the dates, the instances of the murder were typical Coy.)

Coy was riding his horse near his home in Floresville one day when, out of the blue, shots rang out. One shot went through Coy's hat and the other scraped his shoulder. It was just a flesh wound, but it was sore. Coy rode home and had his wife, Manuela, clean and dress the wound. The pain subsided, and after a short rest Coy put on his hat and headed for the fireplace, where his Winchester rifle rested on the mantle.

"Where are you going? You can't leave. What about your shoulder?" his wife implored.

"My shoulder is fine and so am I," Juan replied as he headed out the door. "I need to catch the dog that did this to me."

Coy knew the man and where he would be. The man was in the saloon when Coy strode in with his rifle. The man froze while others in the saloon scattered. The gamblers in the back never noticed.

"Please, I didn't mean it," begged the man as Coy leveled the rifle at him. "Tovar paid me. He wants you dead. He's the—"

Coy pulled the trigger and the man clutched his chest without saying another word. He dropped to the floor—dead.[6]

A month later, Coy was heading to a dance west of San Antonio when a friend told him that two of the deceased man's brothers were lying in wait for him and were armed. Coy went back to San Antonio, bought a box of shells for his Winchester at the first store he came to on North Flores Street, and went to where the two men were hiding.[7]

Back at the original spot, Coy circled around—and sure enough, both brothers were hiding out in the brush. Their horses were tied up to trees not far away. The two men were concentrating on the trail so much they didn't notice Coy sneak up on them.

"*Amigos,* waiting on someone?" Coy called out. He had his Winchester pointing straight at their torsos.

"What the. . . ," one called out as he wheeled around to catch a last glimpse of Coy shooting him in the chest. The other brother ducked to try and confuse Coy. It didn't work. Coy followed him to the ground and fired just as the man was rising up to shoot. Both men were dead instantly.

Coy returned to San Antonio and surrendered himself to authorities.[8] Apparently the jury thought that even though Coy knew what was going to happen, he should have avoided the confrontation.[9] Coy tried telling the judge that inmates he arrested as an officer of the law could retaliate against him. The judge was not swayed.

Francisco Garza and Juan Coy were accused of murdering Luciano Cantu.[10] This is the first and only mention of Francisco Garza (unless it was the Epitacio Garza who rode in with Coy at the Daileyville shooting).

The June 11, 1878, *San Antonio Daily Herald* reported that the case against "Juan McCoy" was "in order for trial to-day in the District Court. A special venue of sixty jurors has been summoned."[11] The next day's *Herald* reported that the special venire was quashed in the Juan Coy case and "a new venire of sixty special jurors was ordered for the 21st inst."[12]

A jury in case No. 219, *State vs. Juan Coy*, was finally seated Friday morning, June 21, 1878. The jury consisted of Frank Seffel, Wenzel Klass, Anton Schoenart, W. Ruppertzburg, Louis Konkele, August Ladner, A. Carhart, H. Binney, Louis Bergstrom, William Booker, José Cassiano, and Henry Brackenridge.[13]

The trial started Friday afternoon, was adjourned at 7:00 P.M. and scheduled to resume at 9:00 A.M. Saturday.[14]

The June 25, 1878, issue of the *San Antonio Daily Herald* reported that both sides finished presenting their evidence and arguments Saturday evening. The jury retired to their room for the night after receiving the case. They agreed on a guilty verdict of manslaughter in the second degree on Sunday. Coy was sentenced to five years in prison.[15] The case against Garza was dismissed at this time and he was released from custody.[16] The judge ruled from the evidence that Garza was innocent of the charge.[17]

The *Herald* reported on June 28 that twenty-three prisoners convicted during the current district court term left on the H. and T. C. Road for the state prison in Huntsville in charge of Sheriff Corwin.[18] Texas Department of Criminal Justice records noted that Coy was received on Tuesday, July 9, 1878, on a five-year sentence of murder from Bexar County.[19]

The Cantu murder was the only record of Coy being sentenced to jail for any crime. A check of district clerk documents for Bexar, Wilson, and Karnes counties did not reveal any other trials, guilty pleas, or punishment phases for Juan Coy at any time. The Wilson County Courthouse, including its papers, burned in 1884.

Perez wrote in his diary that he asked Coy one day how many people he had killed. Coy responded with ". . . what I remember I have killed 33."[20]

John Wesley Hardin's reign of terror ended the same year as Coy's imprisonment; both were jailed in 1878. Hardin, who started his killing at the tender age of fifteen, murdered at least forty people. Most victims were Union soldiers who were trying to apprehend him.[21] Hardin was responsible for more deaths and was more well known than Coy. The son of a Methodist preacher and named for the founder of the Methodist church, Hardin also served a longer prison sentence than Coy.

Coy improved himself in prison, but only in the fighting area. He sharpened his fighting skills and gained more power by intimidation. Some of the fights Coy got into were not his fault, though, as convicts whom Coy had put away during his law enforcement days or beat up during his drinking nights wanted revenge. The guards realized this and were rather lenient in reporting such offenses. Besides, Coy always managed to take care of himself.

The divisiveness between Anglos and Mexicans was obvious in prison. They dared not cross into each other's territory. Fights erupted frequently and without warning. The prison system was nothing more than a weeding out—by death—of the weaker inmates and a training ground for the stronger ones.

Coy was one of the few gunfighters to go to prison. Others who were caught were just hanged. John Wesley Hardin, acting as his own lawyer, was convicted of murder and talked himself out of a hanging and into a prison term. He was imprisoned from 1878 until 1894.[22] Hardin, who also taught school, studied the law while he was in prison and became a lawyer upon his release.

One killer who wasn't as lucky was William Longley, who was hanged in 1877. Longley remarked before the noose was placed around his neck that "I see a lot of enemies out there, and mighty few friends."[23]

Sam Bass wasn't a killer, but he had gained notoriety as a stagecoach and train robber. He never made more than $100 from a stage heist, so he moved on to trains, where he hauled in $60,000 in his first attempt at the Union Pacific.[24] Bass, who would return one dollar to each of his stagecoach victims so that they could buy a meal, was shot down in 1878 by the Texas Rangers as he was preparing for a bank heist.[25]

Coy's five years in prison were the longest he had gone without a gun in his hand since he was younger than ten years old. His other passion, though, was easily obtainable as inmates still found ways to get alcohol. They had a still, and what they didn't produce could be smuggled in from guards.

Coy became something of a leader around jail and helped calm down some prisoners.

"Did you hear what happened in Washington, D.C.?" a prisoner asked Coy one hot July day in 1881. The man was so excited by the news, he didn't even bother waiting for a reply. "Someone shot the president, and he isn't expected to live."

"Is he Democrat or Republican?" Coy asked.

"President Garfield is a Republican," the man replied.

The men sat in the sweltering box-like cell, sweat dripping from every pore.

"Did the man get caught? I wonder if he'll be in jail as long as me," Coy wondered.

"He was caught, and they'll most likely execute him."

Coy sat in his cell and thought about it for a while. "I guess we all live with the possibility of death by someone else. A president is no different than anyone else. The difference comes in the punishment. I kilt me a no count Mexican, so I got five years. If I'da kilt a negro, I'd probably still be free. If I had kilt an Indian, I'd be a hero."

The two prisoners sat silent for a long time, sweltering under the July sun. Flies buzzed around them, providing the only movement in the still air where the wind didn't dare pass.

"Would you ever kill anyone like a president, Juan?" the prisoner asked.

"Doubtful. I wouldn't have any reason," Coy said after some careful thought. "Maybe, if someone wanted me to, I would, but it would have to be a lot of money."

"Yeah, Booth was stupid for killing Lincoln that close up. You know you're going to get caught."

"I know me and the Prez won't be sitting around drinking," laughed Coy, "so we shouldn't get into a fight."

"And I don't think he'd be taking any of our women either," chuckled the other man.

When Coy finished serving his prison sentence in 1883, there had been several changes in the Industrial Revolution. Thomas

Edison had developed the light bulb and had a power plant supplying electricity to customers in New York. There had been some demonstration of the light bulb in San Antonio, and there were plans to join the electrical world in the next few years. For now, though, San Antonio was still on gas lamps.

Butler was still gathering up land and driving cattle up north while Coy was in prison.

The nation's 102nd birthday in 1878 did not generate as much enthusiasm as planned, according to the June 27, 1878, edition of the *San Antonio Daily Herald*. It reported: "If it was not for the fireman, the Germans, and our colored citizens the Greatest American Birthday would be entirely ignored. Americans are in too much of a hurry to attend to such small matters with the national holiday."[26]

Travel had become faster and easier as railroads replaced stagecoaches for long trips. Trains brought more safety to long distance travel in the West, but Indians and outlaws still posed a danger (although much less than on stagecoaches). Some people still traveled by stagecoach, leaving passengers vulnerable to Indians and robbers. Indians were becoming less of a problem in the West, as they were rounded up and taken to reservations and others were wiped out by the U.S. Army.

The Coy family had a couple of oil lamps, but the fireplace still provided the central source for heat, light, and cooking in their small cabin. Although the prison had provided shelter and meals for Coy, he still preferred sleeping under the stars and hunting for his food out in the open. He enjoyed the comfort of home with a bed, a roof, and three home-cooked meals a day, but it took some adjusting once he was free.

Manuela Coy, Juan's wife, left him while he was in prison. The Butlers and Jacobo Coy's family cared for the children. Juan Coy returned from prison to find an empty and quiet house. He saw the children often but didn't know that much about rearing them, so they stayed with the Butlers and Trinidad Coy.

Coy went to the extreme when he gained his freedom, wandering aimlessly from bar to bar for a while and not going home until days later. Besides the absence of freedom, the things he missed most were hunting and fishing.

Coy drank his way up to San Antonio and found the city had

changed some with new buildings and more traffic. Any group of people were strangers to him after his time in prison.

The discussions Coy heard around town surprised him. He had heard about big cities such as New York, Chicago, and Washington before, but the activities in those cities were news to him. The Brooklyn Bridge was completed in New York in 1883 and the first skyscraper reaching ten stories was built in Chicago that same year. The tallest building in San Antonio was still only three stories.

The entertainment world had seen the addition of Buffalo Bill Cody's Wild West Show, which interested Coy. He hoped to see the great western show complete with Annie Oakley. He wanted to compare shooting styles but never had the opportunity.

The motorcycle roared into San Antonio in the late 1880s. Coy heard about the commotion the strange two-wheeled contraption made downtown. The thing belched smoke and a frightful noise as it spun in circles in front of the Alamo and scared horses. Many people considered the ugly machine an evil creature, and some even wanted them banned.

The modern times were coming to San Antonio thanks to motorcycles, but the outlying areas were still busy with horses. The town had a problem with people riding their horses or horse and buggies recklessly, as evidenced by a July 3, 1886, story in the *San Antonio Daily Light*. Albert Phannestein, after several continuances, was fined $5 for careless driving.[27]

"One of the crying evils of the city is the notorious fact of careless or reckless driving, in the streets and it should be promptly put a stop to by the city authorities," reported the *Daily Light*.[28]

Progress took some getting used to, but it was continuing.

CHAPTER FIVE

The Butlers and the Death of Helena

Despite being a legend in Karnes County, William G. Butler had problems with his children that any father of any era would have. Children can always be rebellious and stubborn, and Butler's were no different.

Emmett, Butler's eighteen-year-old son, grew up to be the typical hard-working, hard-drinking ranch hand. He had already been in trouble with the law in Helena and other towns in the area.[1]

One story was told that Sheriff Edgar Leary had made enemies with the Butler family when Leary suspected Emmett of stealing horses and was searching everywhere for the boy. Leary barged into one of the Butler girls' rooms because he thought Emmett might be hiding under the bed.[2]

Mrs. Butler was very upset because her daughter was ill at the time and she didn't appreciate such rude treatment. William Butler was away during the incident, but his wife swore her husband would have words with Leary upon his return, even though the two men were friends.

Another story had it that a Sheriff Risinger was looking for Emmett in connection with stealing horses. There is no word on what happened, except that Risinger left the ranch and immediately resigned as sheriff.[3]

William Butler's house was full of life with eight children.
(Photo courtesy of Charlotte Nichols)

Work on the Butler ranch ceased for the Christmas holidays in 1884, and Emmett enjoyed the holidays with a bottle of whiskey. He had hitched up his horse when his father called out to him that Friday morning, the day after Christmas.

"Stay out of Helena since you're drinking," warned the elder Butler. "The sheriff may be a friend of mine, but I'm not getting you out of any more trouble that you cause there. You are on your own, so just watch it."

From his Kenedy house, the young Butler rode north toward Panna Maria but stopped halfway at the McClane house.[4] The McClanes were family friends and were aware of the friction between Sheriff Edgar Leary and Emmett Butler. The McClanes knew that Bill Butler and the sheriff were friends, so they tried to keep Emmett at the house, even offering him lunch. McClane tried to talk the obviously drunk Butler into going home or staying with them and sleeping it off. Butler adamantly refused and continued on his way toward Panna Maria.[5]

A strange relationship existed among the Anglo Butlers, the Mexican Coys, and the Polish families from Panna Maria. The Butlers and Coys helped the Poles when they were first establishing their town in the 1850s, and the friendship continued to flourish. The two families helped the Poles by providing food and building shelter during the first bone-chilling winter.[6] The Butlers and Coys were accepted as family by the Polish people.

Emmett, who had also made friends through the years thanks to his father, was welcome in Panna Maria and shared in some holiday spirit, which naturally included more liquor. Emmett drank his holiday cheer and enjoyed some of the Polish sausage, then said his good-byes. He unhitched his horse and headed toward Helena, getting drunker at each stop.

Emmett had to steady himself on his horse several times. He saw some squirrels while riding on the trail and squeezed off a couple of shots just to feel the power of the gun in his hand. He was eighteen years old, the son of one of the richest and most popular men in South Texas, and one day he would share 100,000 acres and thousands of cattle with his brothers and sisters.

Helena was the county seat of Karnes County and a crossroads of major trails leading from Mexico and the Gulf of Mexico up north to San Antonio. The town had its own college, a school, the Helena Union Church, a drug store, a saddle and harness shop, two hotels (the American Hotel and the Butler House),[7] two newspapers, a livery stable, mercantile stores, a post office, and, unfortunately, at least thirteen saloons.[8] Being at a crossroads with that many saloons turned the normally peaceful town into a wild and raucous free-for-all on weekends.

Different versions of the incident which followed have appeared in print—then and now. Even the December 30, 1884, issue of the *Daily Express* offered different details and dates on the shooting. The incident is still discussed today as a 1995 issue of *True West* magazine featured a story on the shooting. Situations still exist which may or may not have been the long-term consequences of the shootings.

As noted in the December 31, 1884, issue of the *San Antonio Daily Express,* "The people here are non-committal about the affray, and it is very hard to get the facts in the case, even a perusal of the evidence, given at the inquest is very unsatisfactory, but the facts are essentially as follows:[9]

"As is the custom in country towns during the holidays, many were indulgent in whiskey too freely, and E.W. Butler and Hugh McDonald both were disarmed of their Winchesters by the sheriff," according to the *Daily Express* correspondent. "They were under the influence of whiskey and inclined to be quarrelsome. The sheriff followed them with a posse to arrest them when Butler wheeled around and, with a six-shooter which was previously concealed under his coat, fired at the sheriff, shooting him in the region of the heart and killing him almost instantly. After being shot Leary (the sheriff) said to his posse: 'He has killed me! Shoot him!' and then expired. The dying sheriff, his posse, and it is supposed, others fired at Butler, who had mounted and was riding away. Three shots took effect, one through his brain and two in his right leg below the knee. Butler was shot at 3:40 P.M. and died at one o'clock the next morning. It is said that fully forty shots were fired."[10]

Leary had gone to arrest Butler in connection with the killing of Manuel Lopez during the summer, according to the December 30, 1884, issue of the *Daily Express*. It was alleged that Emmett and a brother shot and killed Lopez in a pasture near Panna Maria following a dance. The town was divided on Butler's status in the killing and he was not arrested until the afternoon following Christmas.[11]

One version of the incident has it that Emmett was angry with Lopez because he "was going to marry a white girl of German descent."[12]

Risinger, sheriff at the time of the Lopez killing, was supposedly threatened if he didn't pursue Butler for murder.[13] The newspaper reported that Risinger received written notice that he must resign or face severe consequences. He resigned.[14]

Another story has the fateful events beginning with McDonald fighting a bar customer, which caused the sheriff's arrival.[15] McDonald, twenty-two years old, was a laborer in the Pleas Butler household in 1880.[16] Emmett was talking with Deputy Sheriff Joe Manning, this story continues, at the time Leary was sought. Emmett, who was holding a rifle, saw Leary through a window and remarked: "Now, he's a bad hombre, ain't he?"[17]

Leary told the crowd that he would enter the saloon, force Butler and McDonald out, and the crowd was to grab McDonald and Butler when they left the saloon. McDonald was the first to leave and he was quickly apprehended by the crowd. Butler, who was still inside polishing his rifle and looking menacingly at Leary, finally walked outside. No one laid a hand on Butler, and Emmett kept walking.[18]

Leary walked out, saw that Butler was still free, and yelled: "Why in hell didn't you catch him?"[19]

Leary pulled his gun and called for Butler to stop. Butler whirled around with his rifle leveled straight at Leary and shot him in the heart.[20]

Butler backed away with the rifle now trained on the crowd, which had drawn their pistols and rifles. The crowd looked in stunned silence. Butler ordered the crowd to release McDonald, but Hugh declined, sensing the impending danger. McDonald did yell at Emmett: "Run, Emmett. You've killed the sheriff."[21]

Butler took the advice and started for his horse as the crowd started firing. Both horses were hit, and Butler jumped on the one with the least amount of wounds.[22]

"He made it about 100 yards up the lane when a bullet struck him in back of his head, going through and lodging just over one of his eyes," according to Maxine Yeater Linder's "Wofford Crossing Road."[23] He was also hit twice in the leg, and died at approximately 2:00 the next morning.[24]

Maxine Linder reported that William Butler arrived in Helena on Monday, the day after Emmett was buried.[25] Notes on Karnes County history, however, say that William Butler was on a cattle drive at the time and had to be summoned back.[26]

The Butler family was powerful in the area. Lawmen began patrolling the streets shortly after the shooting, and tensions ran high as both factions had equal numbers out on the Helena streets.[27] William Butler and Juan Coy rode into town to collect Emmett and bring him home for a proper burial.

Lieutenant Scott and two other Rangers left Yorktown almost immediately upon hearing of the shooting and rode to Helena in the dark and rain to keep peace. Scott shut down the saloons and made provisions for the safety of the men involved in killing Butler. Scott then met with William Butler, who promised him that he and his group of men were not looking for trouble.[28] Butler left shortly after 2:00 P.M. Saturday and his men followed him back to the ranch.[29]

There were different stories on the Emmett Butler killing, but the most important fact about Helena was whether William Butler retaliated against the town or not. The first version swore that Butler wanted revenge against Helena for killing his son. That has the strongest possibility. Another version stated that William Butler realized the mistake his son made in Helena and never retaliated, especially economically. The father was still disturbed by the events and had a hard time holding back his emotions.

Another version held that Emmett Butler wasn't even in a saloon and that there had been no confrontation with the sheriff. This story had it that "a gang of drunks shot up a saloon, and one of their stray bullets killed a man (Emmett Butler) on the street."[30] William Butler buried his son that Sunday, "then rode into Helena the next day with twenty-five armed ranch hands."[31] Butler and his men rode up and down the nearly deserted streets, demanding that his son's killer or killers surrender to him. "By then most of the rowdies had left town, so the colonel's shrill demands echoed on the silent street. Finally, the anguished, frustrated father shouted as he rode away, 'All right! Then I'll kill the town that killed my son!'"[32]

This version continued that Butler lobbied for the rail connection.[33] Butler offered Benjamin Franklin Yoakum, the traffic engineer, the free right-of-way through his ranch but with one stipulation: the railroad must be far west of the San Antonio River and Helena.[34] Thomas Ruckman learned of Butler's offer and raised $32,000, but it was short of the railroad's requested $35,000 and Yoakum had already accepted Butler's offer.[35]

The line was built in 1886 on the other side of the San Antonio River, seven miles west of Helena. The Ox-Cart Road was soon abandoned and two new towns, Kenedy and Karnes City, began growing. A year later, Kenedy became the roundup station for cattle grazing on the open range.[36] By 1892, Karnes City became a railway shipping point on the new line and was the largest town in the county in 1893.[37]

Yet another version had the young Butler and McDonald drinking in the saloon and Leary coming to arrest McDonald, then returning for Butler. With McDonald in custody, Leary tried to arrest Emmett, who backed out of the saloon and shot Leary through the heart.[38]

It is not known why Leary was arresting McDonald, unless he was mistaken for a brother or was in trouble of his own accord.

Before Leary died, he called for the others to capture Butler. Some of the crowd fired upon Emmett and even managed to break his leg. Butler was able to hop on a horse and ride away but with more men continuing in pursuit. The men shot Butler, who fell from his horse and died a short while later.[39]

"The horse came back near the saloon," read the newspaper, "and also fell dead."[40]

Another story had Emmett riding into town and drinking alone at the saloon. He wasn't approached by Leary until after making such a big scene in the saloon. One of the patrons recognized the boy and hurried over to the sheriff's office. Leary sighed because the boy had been warned to stay out of Helena. Leary and the elder Butler had been friends for years and they respected each other. Butler knew Leary was just doing his job in the previous run-ins with Emmett.

"Dammit, Bill, you're a good friend and richer than anyone around here but I try to be fair to everyone and Emmett was causing trouble," Leary explained when Butler came to bail his son out of jail. "He gets drunk and he gets wild. There's no controlling him. When he's sober, he's fine. When he's with you, he's fine. But drunk, forget it. I just hope this doesn't affect our friendship, Bill."

"I know. I understand your predicament. I'll try to keep him under control or at least out of town. I know you have a job to do and I always respect your judgment. Don't worry about our friendship. It's something I value, no matter what my son does."

Leary looked at the pistol comfortably holstered and hanging on a hook in his office. He left the pistol in his office and confronted Emmett unarmed.[41] The bar patron followed close behind as Leary and Deputy Sheriff Risinger strolled across the street to the saloon. The patron waited outside the saloon a few seconds so as not to be fingered as the snitch.

"Emmett, you know what your dad and I have said about you being in town drunk like you are," Leary told Emmett as he approached his table. "Hand over your pistol and go sleep it off."

"No thanks," Emmett said, pulling out his gun and gently squeezing the trigger.[42] Leary never suspected any harm. He was dead before he even hit the floor. Emmett jumped out of the chair, raced outside, and mounted his horse. The violent act also caught Risinger off guard. He had been standing near the bar at the opposite end of the entrance. Risinger ran after Emmett and drew a bead on him before he had a chance to get the horse galloping. Other citizens saw the shooting and went outside with pistols drawn. Risinger and the others took aim and shot. Emmett fell from the horse—dead.[43]

Word circulated around the small town quickly about the sheriff being shot to death as well as his assailant. Risinger also knew the Butlers and wired Kenedy to notify Bill Butler that his son had been killed after killing the sheriff.

Butler was enjoying his holiday with his family when word arrived at his house. He hugged his wife as she silently wept with the younger children.

"The fool," William G. Butler muttered under his breath. "I warned him a hundred times. This will truly be a sorrowful holiday. In the beginning, we were gathering for joy. Now we will gather for sorrow. I'm sorry, honey. I'll go get him so he can be buried here."

Mrs. Butler dabbed her eyes as she held her other children tightly. "Yes, Bill, thank you."

William Butler grabbed his hat and donned his jacket. The coat was difficult to put on as Butler's shoulders sagged from carrying the burden of an entire family. Butler stepped outside and suddenly felt a shiver, not from the weather but from his son's death.

"Juan . . . Juan Coy!" Butler called. Coy appeared from the barn across the way. "Hitch my wagon and saddle your horse. We're riding to Helena. Emmett has been killed and we need to bring him home."

"I'll get my rifle, too, Mr. Butler," Coy announced.

"That's not necessary," Butler said. "There is no confrontation. He killed a sheriff and a deputy returned fire. I know Leary and he would not have provoked this."

The elder Butler got in his wagon and sorrowfully started the long, hard and unpleasant ride to Helena to claim his son so he could be buried on the family property. Butler had warned his son about getting drunk and going to Helena. He knew the sheriff and knew that there was no provocation on his part. Emmett had done something and pulled the trigger first. His son and his friend—both killed at Christmas time.

"Juan, I loved my son, but whiskey got the best of him. He was uncontrollable," Butler said. "But he's my son, and you love them no matter what."

"I know. Sometimes, it doesn't matter how much you discipline them, it's not going to work. Children are stubborn, but I guess they learn it from us," said Coy, who was more like Emmett with the bottle and temper than the elder Butler. "My boys have gotten into their share of trouble. You want life better for your children and will do anything to get it for them."

"This is not a pleasant holiday," Butler said out of the blue. "This is a most difficult task. I saw many men die in the war and in gunfights since then, but when it's your own child, well . . ."

"I'm sorry," Coy said softly, not really knowing what to say. He had killed men before but without much thought about the people left behind. Some of Coy's victims were killed in the line of law enforcement, some were from fights or being provoked, and others Juan killed while protecting Butler's land or property. That was one of his duties in working for Mr. Butler.

The ride was quiet as Butler mourned his son's death. Butler found his eyes tearing up from time to time as he stared pensively off in the distance. He glanced up occasionally to ensure that he was still on the trail following Coy.

Butler thought back to when Emmett was just a toddler. He was scared of being around horses, but that was forgotten as soon as his father put him in the saddle with him. He didn't want to get off after that. Emmett was about six or seven when his father took him deer hunting for the first time. The rifle Emmett shouldered was almost as big as him, but he knew what to do until he pulled the trigger and the recoil sent him sprawling.

Butler and Coy reached Helena later that afternoon. Butler went to the sheriff's office to apologize to Risinger.

"I'd like to offer my condolences to Mrs. Leary, but it's inappropriate at this time. Please give her my condolences and this money to help out." Butler placed two gold coins on the table. "If she needs anything, please let me know."

"She'd appreciate the gesture, Mr. Butler," Risinger said. "This is not a good holiday for either family. I had no choice, Mr. Butler, I'm sorry."

"I know, Emmett was not responsible when he was drinking. He was the best son on my ranch but the worst in a bar. Can I get him now? His mother is waiting on us."

"I already sent a couple of men to place him in your wagon, sir. They should be finished."

"Thank you . . . thank you very much, Sheriff."
"Please pass my condolences to your family."

Butler nodded at the new sheriff and slowly rose out of the chair. He stood up but his shoulders slumped forward. There was no effort about him as he walked outside and climbed aboard the wagon. He glanced in the back and noticed the blanket covering his son. There were blood stains at the head and the legs.

The ride back was long. Butler and Coy didn't return until night had already set. Mrs. Butler was waiting on the porch.

The obituary for Leary was printed in the December 31, 1884, issue of *The Daily Express*: "Edgar Leary was claimed by many to have been the best sheriff that Karnes County has ever had, and while some question his discretion, all agreed that he never feared to go where duty called him. He was the only sheriff Karnes County ever had who rigidly enforced the six-shooter law."[44]

Since no one had applied for the job as of the December 31 issue, the county commissioners postponed any decisions for a week, in hopes of receiving some applicants.[45]

"As the county is divided into two factions it will be hard to find a man to fill the sheriff's office whose sympathy is not with one of them, and several prominent citizens wish Lieutenant Scott, of the rangers, to accept the office, but as the income is small he is not likely to accept," the newspaper continued. "At present he is virtually sheriff and much admiration is expressed for his efforts, in averting trouble today."[46]

It was believed by many that when William Butler arrived in Helena, he vowed to kill the town that killed his son. Butler didn't do anything just then but years later, when the railroad wanted to build a line in South Texas, he gave the railroad land and money to change their route from Helena to Kenedy.

Emmett was not the first Butler to be killed on the Helena streets. His uncle, Wash, was involved in a shootout a few years earlier with John Cooper, and both men were killed instantly.[47]

Emmett was the second oldest son. The 1880 census showed Newton at age twenty-one already married to Mary A. Butler, twenty-three years old, and father of Effie May, a one-year-old girl, and an unnamed two-month-old son who was born in March 1880.[48] Newton died on March 12, 1895.[49]

The 1880 census showed the other Butler children were still

single. All eight children were born in Texas. Their father was born in Mississippi and their mother in Ohio. Helen was twenty years old, Louissa was eighteen, Emmett was sixteen at the time, Sykes was thirteen, Cora was ten, Theodore, eight, and William G., Jr., was three years old. William, Jr., died on November 20, 1913. Emmett was the only single child who was not at home at the time of the census. He was away at school. The 1880 census also showed Ned Potter residing at the Butler house. He was an eighteen-year-old single black servant, born in Texas.[50]

Helena, the county seat for Karnes County, was a prosperous town. It was established in 1852 by Thomas Ruckman, who thought the area at the crossroads would make a good town.[51] The town was first known as Alamita and consisted of only a small store and a blacksmith shop. Karnes County was established on February 4, 1854, out of Bexar, Gonzalez, DeWitt, Goliad, and San Patricio counties. Thirty years later, Helena had a population of over 500 people. On Saturday nights there were many more people, as the saloons held most of the visitors.

Saturdays were busy days and provided much excitement around town, whether it was a dance for the locals or a night of drinking for the workers. The important court cases were held on Saturdays, because they provided entertainment for the citizens. Families traveled for miles to visit Helena in hopes of witnessing a hanging. They brought picnic lunches to watch the legal proceedings on the second floor of the courthouse, and were most interested in the punishment phase of the trial. The jail, which was a small, metal box with just enough room for one person to stand, sat just yards away from the white courthouse and the post office. The court was packed with visitors who usually hoped for a guilty verdict. There wasn't much time for appeal, as many guilty verdicts, which resulted in a death penalty, were carried out that very afternoon across the street from the courthouse.

Helena was a key town in South Texas in those days, being a major crossroads for shipping routes from the north and south and less than a day's ride from the port city of Indianola. More than a dozen saloons in town were constantly filled on weekends with hard-drinking, hard-living cattlemen and freighters. The alcohol flowed freely, which led to fights, shootouts, and a unique kind of duel.

A brutal type of killing had its origins in Helena and was called

The Helena Courthouse as it is today. The bottom floor now houses a museum.

the Helena Duel.[52] Two fighting men settled their differences with knives in a treacherous way, even for the Wild West. The combatants lashed their left wrists together with leather while holding three-inch knives in their right hands. The knives were just long enough to inflict serious damage but not big enough to cause instant death. The loser was slashed to pieces and died a slow, agonizing death from the loss of blood.[53]

Not everything about Helena was brutal, though. The city was one of just seven Texas cities to issue its own stamp during the Civil War.[54] Helena citizens raised money after the Civil War to build a college, the Helena Academy.[55] The college stayed in operation approximately twenty years.

Cattle drives were becoming more and more obsolete by the 1880s. Barbed wire was changing the way cattle ranching had been done over the years. Ranchers were digging post holes and installing barbed wire for roping off and denying access to territories and passageways that had been used for years in cattle drives. It

The tiny Helena jail cell sits out on the grounds across from the courthouse.

was much easier to install barbed wire than the wooden fences which were used for near the barn and on the corral. All the barbed wire fencing took was digging a hole, placing a post in the ground, wrapping the wire around the post, and stretching it out to the next post. More and more farmers were fencing off their property to keep cattlemen and sheepherders from having free grazing rites to their land. It kept cattle in a set boundary and prohibited rustlers from just taking cattle off the trail. Rustlers still prospered, but the wire fence made it a little harder for them to operate.

The Wild West's landscape was changing because of the

progress of railroads and cattle ranching. It is believed Butler tried to keep pace with those changes when it came time for the proposed rail line.

The San Antonio and Aransas Pass Railroad wanted to pass through Karnes County, specifically Helena, with its new line. The railroad asked the Helena citizens for $35,000 in cash and the property where the tracks would run. Many of the citizens, looking to the future, agreed with the request—but not enough complied.[56] Helena fell less than $5,000 short of the $35,000 needed despite the railroad giving them extra time.

Butler kept track of the negotiations and urged the town to raise the money, but with no luck. The railroad's second choice was Butler's property, and when all efforts had been exhausted with the Helena citizens Butler donated the necessary land and money.[57]

Many people claimed that Butler's decision to donate some of his land to the railroad, thereby rerouting it from the proposed Helena passage, was retaliation for his son's death in Helena. The move benefited Butler greatly, as he cut costs and turned the money around much quicker since the cattle went to Kansas and Abilene on the rail in a few days instead of weeks by land.

Butler always said—and the financial records backed him up—that the reasons for donating the land were purely in the interest of business. He saved money on his cattle operation, and the land value around the railroad increased. Butler was a shrewd businessman with good foresight to understand such ramifications.[58] Some of that land had belonged to the Coys, who had sold it to the Butlers years earlier. Butler upheld his promise and continued to support the Coys.

The town of Helena began to die. On December 21, 1893, the county voted to move the county seat from Helena to Karnes City.[59] The vote was 862 for Karnes City and 120 to stay in Helena.[60] But Helena government officials refused to abide by the election and did not cooperate in the transfer of county records and documents to the new county seat.

One night, officials from Karnes City guided twenty wagons to the county offices in Helena and packed documents, desks, and anything else official for the trip to Karnes City. Helena hired an armed guard to protect the documents and other official county items.[61] The guard never fired a shot or tried to stop anyone but instead hopped aboard the wagon train for the short trip.

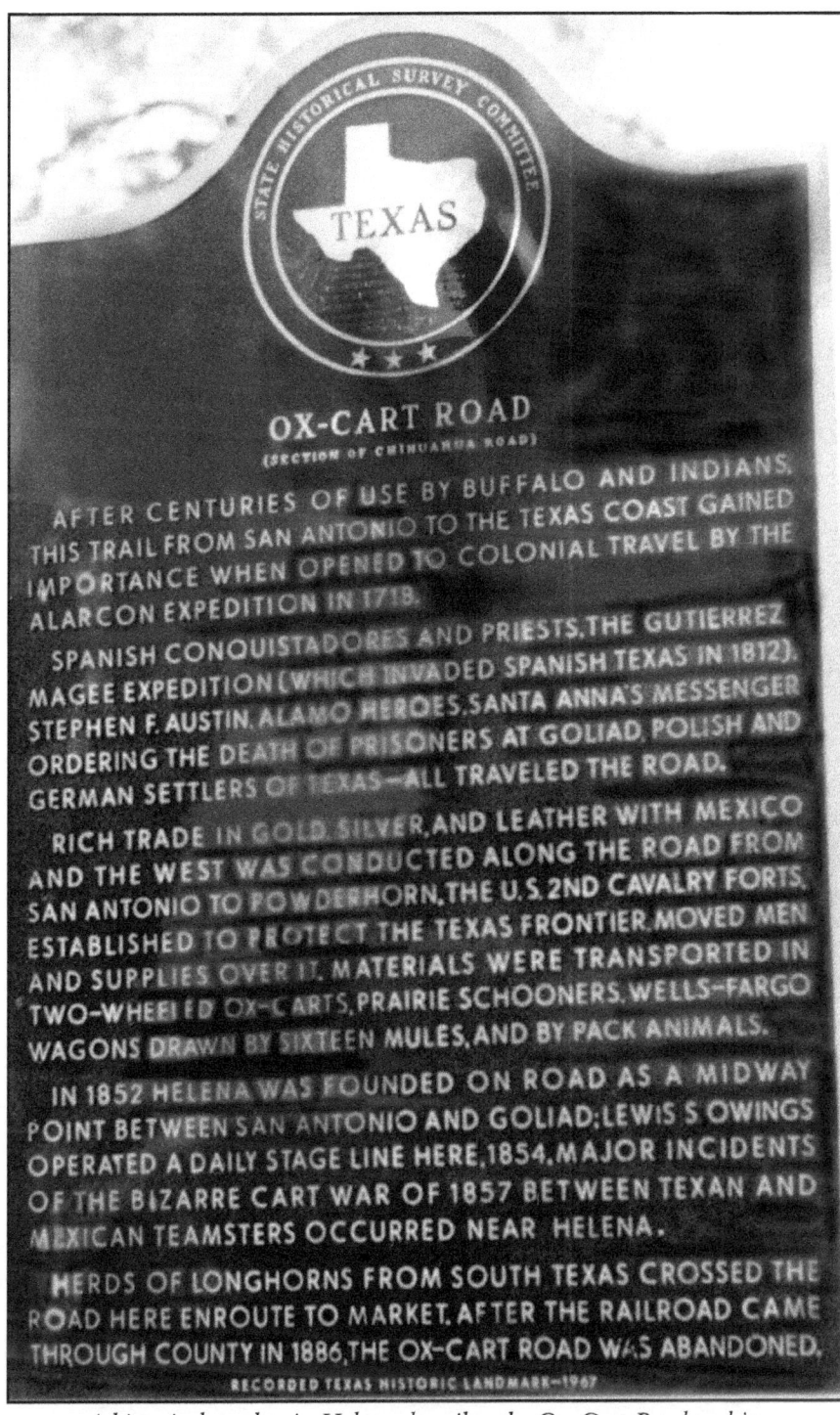

A historical marker in Helena describes the Ox-Cart Road and its importance to the area.

The Helena Post Office, which issued its own stamps during the Civil War, still stands today.

Asked later why he didn't shoot the intruders, the quick-witted man replied, "That wasn't my order. I was told to guard the records, which I did."

Helena, which was such a booming town in the 1880s, deteriorated to almost nothing in the 1890s.

Today, Helena is home to fewer people (approximately 100 total) than in its heyday back in the 1880s. The only remnants of the old town are the courthouse, the post office, the Ruckman House, the Carver-Mayfield store, and the Masonic Lodge, which are all owned by the Karnes County Historical Society.[62] Even today, the courthouse, which houses the museum, is under threat of closure by public officials.

HELENA

FOUNDED IN 1852 ON SAN ANTONIO RIVER BY THOMAS RUCKMAN, A GRADUATE OF PRINCETON, AND LEWIS OWINGS LATER FIRST GOVERNOR OF ARIZONA TERRITORY. TOWN WAS NAMED IN HONOR OF OWINGS' WIFE, HELEN.

SITUATED ON BRANCH OF FAMED CHIHUAHUA TRAIL (RUNNING FROM INDIANOLA TO SAN ANTONIO TO NORTHERN MEXICO), HELENA WAS TO EXPERIENCE QUICK GROWTH. MUCH TRAFFIC OF WAGON FREIGHT AND GOLD BULLION TRAVELED TRAIL. FOUR-HORSE STAGES DAILY PASSED THROUGH TOWN.

HELENA WAS DESIGNATED COUNTY SEAT WHEN KARNES COUNTY WAS CREATED AND ORGANIZED IN 1854. FIRST ELECTION OF COUNTY OFFICIALS WAS HELD ON GALLERY OF RUCKMAN-OWINGS STORE.

DURING CIVIL WAR, KARNES COUNTY MUSTERED SIX COMPANIES, INCLUDING HELENA GUARDS, FOR SERVICE. HELENA WAS A CONFEDERATE POST OFFICE AND ISSUED ITS OWN STAMPS. MUCH CONFEDERATE COTTON DESTINED FOR MEXICAN PORTS PASSED THROUGH HELENA.

DURING ITS HEYDAY, HELENA HAD A COURTHOUSE, JAIL, NEWSPAPER, ACADEMY, DRUGSTORE, BLACKSMITH SHOP, TWO HOTELS, AND SEVERAL SALOONS AND GENERAL STORES.

BYPASSED BY THE S.A. & A.P. RAILROAD IN 1886, TOWN DIED. COUNTY SEAT WAS MOVED TO KARNES CITY IN 1894 AFTER HOTLY CONTESTED ELECTION.

(1967)

A historical marker explains the beginnings of Helena.

Chapter Six

A Little Less Work and a Lot More Trouble

Juan Coy was more than just a farmhand for William G. Butler. They were old friends, despite the differences in ethnicity and economic class. Butler trusted Coy with his life, his family, and his property. Coy led most of Butler's cattle drives up to Amarillo and on into Kansas. Butler sensed that trains would take the place of cowboys in driving the cattle to market, hence the agreement with the railroad on the land. Not only could he make money on the property value but he would save money, time, and cattle by being near a railroad stop.

"Boss, when are we going back to being cowboys?" Coy asked Butler one day. "I'm supposed to be a *vaquero*, but I do almost nothing now except branding and loading them on the trains."

"It's the way of the future, Juan," Butler replied. "It's cheaper and faster to send the cattle on a train. The cattle get to market quicker and I get more money faster. The bad thing is there are less cowboys on the ranch now."

"That's another thing," Coy started. "What are . . ."

"Juan, I know, I sympathize with you and them," Butler said. "Many of these men were like my family. We have to learn new ways. Some of them are at the other ranch, planting hay and peanuts and doing other work."

"Hay I can see, but I can't understand why peanuts," questioned Coy.

"Trust me," Butler said. "A lot has changed in twenty years. I still remember my first cattle drive up to Abilene in 1868. Me and Seth probably sent up close to 2,000 head of cattle."

The progress of railroads in the 1880s was cutting into the cowboy mystique and the job itself. Butler quit hiring cowboys, and some even left the ranch to find other work. Coy and his relatives were still needed to work the ranch, but one of the main duties was gone. That meant more idle time for Coy.

The introduction of barbed wire in San Antonio in 1876 had also changed the cattle industry. The cattle had a way of charging through some of the smaller, weaker wooden fences that were erected around homes. The barbed wire was stronger, easier, cheaper, and more efficient to handle.

Many cattlemen enjoyed the idea of cattle roaming freely upon open ranges, and they opposed the strands of wire that kept their cattle out of grassy areas. Sometimes there were more than protests as some cattlemen cut the wires. It took some adjustment but soon the cattlemen saw the advantages, mainly that not only did it keep their cattle in but it made the rustlers work a little harder in stealing. No longer could rustlers just ride around, find some free roaming cattle to call their own, and head to market with an easy profit. It didn't stop the rustlers from knocking down the fences to help themselves to cattle, however.

Butler, Coy, and the others all missed the days of driving the cattle to Abilene and experiencing the wild outdoors. Now Butler and Coy both found themselves staying at home more with their families. They enjoyed their families, but they missed the outdoor adventure. They still experienced the old cowboy times when they were rounding up the cattle in preparation to load them on a cattle car or to brand them. They still spent some nights out under the stars, but those nights were fewer and fewer. Butler found himself getting dressed up more often and meeting people over business. Coy also spent more time working as a law enforcement officer. He was still Butler's hired gun, but even that job was needed less frequently.

The Civil War brought criminals, cutthroats, rustlers, and other ne'er-do-wells. Some were soldiers who ran amok during the war and saw no reason to stop the success they had discovered. The crooks were running the town at times as they intimidated judges, juries, and lawyers into not-guilty verdicts if they even got to court. Soon a vigilante group took the law into their own hands, and peace and civility were restored.

Justice through the vigilantes was swift and decisive. One outlaw who had just been declared not guilty after threatening the judge and jury begged to be let back into jail after seeing the mob waiting for him outside the courthouse. Despite his pleadings and protests from Bishop Dubuis, whose chinaberry tree was now the hanging tree, the outlaw was executed in front of a large crowd of adults and children in San Antonio. Bishop Dubuis chopped down all ten chinaberry trees at his residence in front of Military Plaza by the next morning.

Juan Coy avoided such scrutiny because of his relationship with Butler and the fact that he was a law enforcement official. Some of his killings could be attributed to law enforcement work, but several were in that gray area between law enforcement and law breaking.

Being a former law enforcement officer did not save a man accused in the attempted murder of his brother-in-law in Alabama. Former sheriff John Reupoe of Sumpter County, Alabama, was taken from his jail cell and hanged by a mob.[1]

In the progress that hit South Texas in the 1880s, houses were being better constructed. Gone were the days when the house was just the sleeping area with a kitchen in another building separated by a dog trot. People found it to be more convenient to have the kitchen and eating area under the same roof as the sleeping area. There were problems with this arrangement, though, as the houses became very hot in the summer from the cooking. Windows were open, but that was just an invitation for mosquitoes and flies. The new arrangement made it extremely nice in the winter as the fire warmed the house. Sometimes the fire seemed to choke the oxygen out of the room. There were still times when embers popped and started a house fire, but people quickly learned to keep any blankets and straw away from the dirt floor fire area.

Coy used some of his idle time to moonlight in law enforcement, but some of it was spent in saloons. Alcohol consumed Juan Coy. It was his downfall. Drinking led to belligerence, which led to fights. He always won the fights. His build and quick, powerful fists always made him a winner. The situation had Coy on both sides of the law in the same day on more than one occasion.

Because his law enforcement jobs were usually in San Antonio, that's where the majority of drinking—and eventually fighting—occurred. His law enforcement position as well as his cousins Jacobo and Andres Coy helped shield him from some trouble in saloons. Juan slept off many a fight at one of the cousins' houses. When his cousins couldn't get him out of trouble, his old friend, William Butler, did.

"Ooooh, what happened last night?" Juan Coy asked as he groggily picked himself off the floor one morning. His clothes were still on him from the night before and he smelled of whiskey. Jacobo Coy was near the door looking at the sun peek over the trees that lined Matamoros Street.

"You got into another fight and beat up some poor hack," Jacobo Coy replied. "You've got to stop that. You're going to get tossed in jail one time too many and I'm not going to be able to get you out. Provided I want to get you out."

"If I won, why does my head hurt so much?" Juan asked.

"You were on the verge of killing the poor guy when I knocked you out with my pistol," Jacobo said as he displayed the gun. "Save it for the criminals."

"You son of a bitch." Juan Coy rose quickly and approached his cousin in a less than family way. Jacobo knew what was coming and slowly turned around for Juan to see a cocked pistol pointing straight at his abdomen.

"Hold off, Juan," Jacobo said. "The captain said when you straighten out, he'll put you back on the payroll. So I guess it's best for you to head back to Kenedy. I've wired Mr. Butler."

Juan Coy stood silently, looking at the pistol. He wouldn't hurt his cousin. Maybe he'd just punch him in the stomach, but it would be nothing serious. Besides, he was sober now and this was family. He only fought when he got drunk—and never his own family. His fights were always against strangers, someone who provoked him and deserved it.

"One of these days, Juan, you will regret the reputation you have tried so hard to build," Jacobo warned. "You are feared and dangerous and have won many a good fight. But one day, someone will stand up to you and say *no more*."

Juan did not say anything. He looked at Jacobo and wondered why he and Andres were always preaching to him. They were just like him at one time, on the wrong side of the law more often than being on the right side. Juan had calmed down and become more respectable, but he couldn't find a reason to totally convert. He enjoyed the intimidation he held over others.

Coy was a dangerous man when he wasn't drinking but even worse when he had been at a saloon all night, which was often. It helped that he had relatives on the San Antonio police force and true friends such as the Butler family, but sometimes his connections couldn't keep him out of trouble. There was no trying to reason with the man, especially if liquor was nearby.

Coy used his fists for law enforcement purposes on many occasions, usually in helping family members who were fellow officers. Coy's cousin, Jesse Perez, wrote in his diary about having to arrest two men for the Von Ormy justice of the peace. Perez arrested one man and sent the other man to the judge, who arrested him. Both men were fined $17.[2]

"We know who you are and we're going to get that $17 back from you," threatened one man. "Every last drop."

Perez managed to avoid the two. One Saturday, Juan Coy came to visit for a few days. Coy and Perez went to a dance and along the way Perez told his older cousin about the fine and the threat. Coy assured Perez that he had nothing to fear; he would be there if an altercation broke out. Sure enough, Perez saw one of the men, who reminded him about the $17 fine and how he was going to avenge the matter. The man approached Perez but Perez was quicker as he knocked the man on the head, just in back of the ear, and down he went. Coy joined in whipping the man some more after he was down. Perez arrested him and took him before the judge, who fined him an additional $5.[3]

Shortly after that incident, Coy offered Perez a job on the Honey Ranch, William Butler's spread in Karnes County. Coy introduced Perez to Butler, telling him that he was Tom Perez' son. Butler hired him for $25 a month plus a place to sleep and three meals a day. Coy told him to stay with Butler to handle his odd jobs around the house, which included taking off Butler's boots and bringing him coffee.[4]

After Perez had been there a week, one of the black farm

workers picked a fight with him. Perez avoided the altercation and told him he was there to work, not fight, and he didn't want Butler getting the wrong idea about him. Unbeknownst to Perez, though, Butler ordered Bill Sanders, the black worker, to pick a fight with Perez to test his mettle. Perez, who was just seventeen years old at the time and probably stood only 5'5, told Sanders, who was twenty-two years old and 6', he would fight him someday. It came early enough. One morning, Perez was carrying a stack of wood when Sanders again confronted him. Perez dropped the wood save for one piece that he held in his right hand and hit Sanders in the head, knocking him down. Sanders recovered quickly and knocked Perez above the left eye, sending him to the ground. Suddenly, Butler appeared, asking for coffee, much to Perez' relief. Perez knew Sanders was on the verge of closing his other eye with another punch.[5]

Later that afternoon, Butler told Sanders to bring his horse around and hitch it to the buggy. While Sanders went to get the horse, Perez got a shotgun and loaded it with rock salt. Perez followed Sanders and shot him from behind at long range. Sanders turned around and Perez fired again. Sanders jumped the fence and took off running for help. Perez headed back to the house, where Butler waited for him. Butler asked for more coffee and while Perez got it for him, Butler wondered aloud where Sanders was with the horse. It had been an hour and still no sign of him. Jim, the other black worker, told Butler "that little Mexican shot old Sanders' ass of(f)."[6] A week later, after Sanders recuperated, Coy tried to get Sanders to pick another fight with Perez. Sanders declined the offer, having learned his lesson the first time.[7]

On one of the last cattle drives, Sykes Butler, Coy, Perez, and others left the Honey Ranch with 1,200 steers in March 1886 bound for Dodge City, Kansas. They sold 800 head of cattle in Dodge City, then took the remaining 400 head to sell in St. Louis. The Midwest city had never seen many Mexicans, and Perez became something of a novelty. He hooked up with three men who took him to variety shows. At one theater he was surrounded by twenty girls, who inquired about his nationality and how his hair became so black.

"Oooh, he's just so good looking with all of that black hair," one girl gushed. "I want to run my fingers all over it."

The youthful Perez ate up all of the attention while Butler and Coy laughed at the entire scene. They had seen it before.

Butler, Coy, Perez, and the others went back to Kansas, where Butler bought a race horse for $450.[8] They returned to the Honey Ranch, but Sykes Butler went back to Dodge City a month later to check on the steers. While Butler was gone, Coy suggested to Perez they take the race horse to Floresville and run it against another horse. Perez warned Coy about stealing and how Sykes Butler would probably throw him in jail for taking the horse.[9] Coy convinced him Butler wouldn't know a thing about it. Perez gathered $86 to bet, but Coy was broke. The two were headed for the Conquista Crossing Friday when suddenly William Butler rode up. Coy took the horse into the brush and hid it.[10]

"Hello, Colonel Butler," Coy said as he joined the two men. "Me and Jesse are going to Floresville. Could you give me a hunnert dollars, please sir?"

"Sorry, John," Butler replied. "I don't have anything on me and I don't have my checkbook with me."

"Wait right here," Coy said as he walked over to an elm tree and peeled off some white bark. He brought it over to Butler. "You can write it on this."

Butler took the bark, wrote out a check for $100, and handed it to Coy. Perez and Coy waited a bit for Butler to clear out of view before taking off. That night, Coy cashed the piece of bark for $100 at a saloon in Lodi.[11]

People were already filling up the area for the horse races that Saturday when Coy, Perez, and the race horse showed up. Coy had applied mud to the horse to make him look a little worn, giving him more of a plow horse look rather than a race horse. Coy found Monroe and challenged him to a bet. The wagering started at $25 but soon progressed to the $100 Coy had received from Butler. Coy also wagered his horse against Monroe's, which upset Perez.[12]

"John, are you loco? First you steal Butler's horse, then you bet his horse against Monroe's horse. Have you thought about what will happen if you lose? We'll be going to prison. Butler will put us away," Perez tried to reason with his cousin.

"Don't worry," Coy reassured Perez. "Now, go bet your $86 so we can make some more money on this."

Nothing Coy could do would reassure his cousin. Perez was very worried about the whole transaction.

"Coy's been drinking if he's betting on that horse," said one bystander as Perez passed through the crowd to gamble his $86. A few more men went to bet money on the race.

The race started with Monroe's horse in the lead. Perez was riding Butler's horse and soon caught up. Perez heard a gun shot and people started scattering. Another shot rang out and Perez slowed his horse so he could avoid the scrambling people. When he looked around he saw that Coy had gunned down Monroe and was riding Wilson County Sheriff Ximenes' horse.[13]

Coy promised Ximenes he would return the next day with the horse and turn himself in.[14]

Everything went haywire for Perez in such a short time. He and Coy had lost $186 on the deal, and Coy had ridden off with Butler's horse to avoid any more problems. They arrived back at the ranch at 3:00 A.M. and found Butler asleep on his front porch.[15] Butler woke up from the noise of horses panting to see Coy and Perez there. Coy explained the previous day's events and how he had killed Monroe.

"Hitch up my horse and we'll go to Floresville," Butler ordered as he headed for the house to collect $5,000 bond for Coy.[16] "Perez, you stay here."

The activities were nothing new for either Coy or Butler—Coy got in trouble and Butler bailed him out. Butler approved of Coy's reckless abandon because such actions kept people guessing and made it less likely that people would challenge Butler's or Coy's authority. It provided both men strength.

"Mr. Jess," Sanders said as he joined Perez out on the porch. All had been forgiven between the two after Perez learned that Butler had put Sanders up to the attack. "What was the matter with that Nigger Monroe? I just soon commit suicide than to run a race aginst John Coy."[17]

Butler paid the $5,000 bond for Coy and the two headed home. Wilson County indicted Coy for the murder of Monroe, accepted the $5,000 bond, and that was as far as the case went. Coy was still under indictment when he died.

Many men of the era engaged in some form of gambling, whether it was horse racing, cockfights, dice, or cards. Even some women got the gambling fever. Strong religious groups were opposed to gambling and some even to dances. Dances entertained both sexes and people of all ages. Communities staged dances on

Friday and Saturday nights, with some being held in the one-room schoolhouse, the town square, or a town meeting place. Dances were a great social gathering place, but there was always the possibility a fight could break out.

There were five Guzman brothers who attended dances frequently and who also broke them up by starting fights.[18] Perez went to one dance which was attended by the Guzmans and discovered the stories about them were true. Coy went with Perez to the next dance and, sure enough, the Guzmans were there and a small scuffle broke out. Coy was more interested in a certain girl he talked with most of the night. Back at the Honey Ranch, Coy still talked about the girl except on the occasions when he plotted revenge on the Guzmans for interrupting his conversations with her.[19]

Coy told the girl he would meet her at the next week's dance.

"Hoo boy," Perez declared that night after hearing all of Coy's talk. "Dem Guzmans saddling the wrong horse when they jump on John Coy."[20]

When a week had passed and it was time for another dance, Butler warned Coy to stay out of trouble. Coy promised he would. Lanterns hung in each corner of the one-room schoolhouse. Emmett Coy, another of Juan's cousins, accompanied Juan Coy and Jesse Perez to that night's dance.[21]

"Emmett and Jesse, each of you stand by a lantern," Juan Coy instructed his cousins. "If any fighting commences, blow out the lanterns and I'll do the rest."[22]

It wasn't long before the eldest Guzman started something with Juan Coy. Emmett and Jesse followed Juan's directions and the lights went out. A few shots rang out, and soon the lights went back on. Everyone saw the eldest Guzman boy hanging through a window, screaming in pain from gunshot wounds to his arm and his stomach. A second brother was shot in the hip. Both brothers ran off into the brush. The Coys and Perez hid their guns just before the law came asking about gunshots.[23]

"They musta shot each other," Juan Coy said. "It was dark when the fighting commenced. Jesse pushed an old woman and two girls through a window, then I dragged him out."[24]

"I didn't see nothing," Jesse Perez said. "I just pushed everybody when I heard the gunshots."[25]

Perez quit Butler's employ soon after and moved to Elm

Creek on the Garza Crossing road that was sixteen miles south of San Antonio.[26] Perez returned to law enforcement and did some ranching.

That was the last time the Guzmans bothered the area dances. Once again, Coy let his actions settle any problems.

CHAPTER SEVEN

Prejudice Amid Progress

The times were changing in South Texas and the United States in the late 1880s. In Coy's youth, Texans fought Indians, Yankees, Mexicans, and each other with regularity. Peace had been made eventually with every group save for themselves and the Indians.

The Civil War ended in 1865 and Reconstruction lasted for a dozen or so years. The Anglos' treatment of Mexicans improved over time. Prejudice remained, but Anglos and Mexicans were getting along better than the African American and Anglos were. The Ku Klux Klan started after the Civil War, targeting Catholics, Jews, and blacks. San Antonio was a melting pot, with the additional presence of Germans, Poles, Irish, and Chinese. Geronimo and other Indians had been captured while others were pushed further onto reservations. Geronimo was even quartered at Fort Sam Houston for a short time in the fall of 1886.[1]

Despite the overall improvement of race relations as a whole in San Antonio, there were still many individual cases of prejudice. Hispanics were in the majority in San Antonio, with Anglos at about 40 percent and African Americans at less than 10 percent. Still, most of the economic and political power belonged to the Anglos. A survey in the mid-nineteenth century in South and West Texas showed 19.2 percent of the Mexican American population and 47.7 percent of Anglo Americans employed.² The same survey showed 25.1 percent of Mexican Americans as literate and 86.6 percent of Anglo Americans as literate.³ The survey did not include African Americans.

Blacks bore the brunt of the prejudice from Anglos and Mexicans even though there were isolated cases of Anglos against the Mexicans. The few cases of lynching were predominantly against blacks. The Germans thought they were superior to all groups, including Anglos who were not of German descent. The Germans' work ethic was outstanding, and most of the good jobs went to them. They created their own neighborhood, which had traditionally been Mexican. It was near downtown, close enough to stay in touch with the city but far enough away to be away from the trouble. The area was also on the San Antonio River, which was necessary for cleaning, farming, and the Guenther Flour Mill. The San Antonio River became a breeding ground for illness as many people used it for sewerage disposal. Educating the public on the dangers of sewerage disposal took years of work before the river returned to its original function. The river became something of a dividing line for the groups.

Juan Coy enjoyed the night life the city offered but did not like the total atmosphere and the lack of respect for Mexicans. The farm and ranch served as more of an equalizer than the city. Butler knew how important Juan Coy was to him and treated him as such.

Butler and Coy needed each other more and more as time went on. The loyalty between the two not only crossed ethnic and cultural lines but generational as well. They were of the same generation, despite Butler being ten years older. They had grown up on the frontier and had the rough and hard edge to them which younger men don't possess. Coy and Butler had survived tough times during the settlement of South Texas, which the younger generation just took for granted. The younger generation's wild times were spent more on recreational activities, while the older generation's wild times were spent on work. Butler and Coy were of the age that sought to preserve and protect what they had and respect others' property. Now there was more conquest and capture in the fights.

People were determined to protect their property despite the risk involved. Vigilantism grew out of the citizens' frustration with law enforcement, which was weak in dealing with criminals.

Theft and murder led three men to take the law into their own hands on a railroad in June 1886. The June 29, 1886, *San Antonio Daily Light* reported that three armed men boarded the west-bound No. 20 train when it stopped for water at the Cline Station, about 145 miles west of San Antonio.[4] The three men took two Mexicans to the rear of the sleeper car and shot them. One survived long enough to jump from the train and run into the brush. He was captured near the train and killed.[5]

"The parties doing the killing are supposed to be citizens of the vicinity who had lost stock, and that the Mexicans had been stealing the same," reported the *Daily Light*. "The two Mexicans killed are also accused of murder near Uvalde. No arrests have been made."[6]

Butler donated some land to Yoakum's railroad in the 1880s so that track could be laid from the Corpus Christi area to San Antonio. The cattle drive days were becoming a thing of the past. No longer did cowboys spend weeks on the prairie transporting cattle to market. Trains were faster, easier, and cheaper. All that was required to be done was to herd the cattle down to a train depot, load them onto a cattle car, and send them to the stockyards in Fort Worth or Kansas. Fewer ranch hands were needed, and the transaction could be done in just a couple of days instead of a couple of weeks.

The railroad also speeded up the delivery of the mail. The *San Antonio Daily Light* reported June 30, 1886, that the mail would be on the San Antonio and Aransas Pass line as far as Beeville, which would take just nine hours as opposed to the five days on the Victoria route.[7]

Butler recognized the advantage of the railroad early and capitalized on it. He explained the business to Coy, who was involved in it from a law enforcement angle. The railroad provided opportunities for many people as they started businesses near the rail line. The railroad went through Karnes County in 1886, and Kenedy became a roundup station for cattle grazing in 1887. Karnes City became a railway shipping point in 1892.[8]

Butler became unpopular before the railroad was even re-routed to his land. Citizens of Helena were especially resentful of Butler for his land deal with the railroad. Some of Butler's neighbors in Kenedy did not like the railroad either and thought Butler was gaining too much power.

William G. Butler started appearing in civil court during the mid-1880s.⁹ Some cases did not mention any background or details but just reported the outcome. One case in Karnes County on October 16, 1885, was *J. W. Newton v. W. G. Butler*. The defendant's (Butler's) motion to dismiss the case was granted for failure of the prosecution to present its case. The court decreed that plaintiff should recover court costs.¹⁰

The Taylor-Sutton Feud cost many lives in South Texas for fifty years during the 1800s. The Butler family was involved in one of the offshoots of this feud. South Texas was filled with warring factions. Everyone knew what side everyone else was on and what towns were under whose control. Law enforcement officials in some towns were nothing more than hired guns placed there by the head of a warring group. The Texas Rangers were mainly worried about the Indians and did not involve themselves in the local politics that much.

Such was the law back in the 1800s. The law was not enforced across the board because many lawmen were just hired guns of the power brokers in town. Juan Coy dabbled in some local law enforcement jobs but tired of just the minor rules. He enjoyed life on the land, where it was survival of the fittest, despite Butler's pleas to keep up with changes.

"Juan, you know you always have a place with our family," Butler said one night when the two returned from Corpus Christi. They had made the three-day journey to check on cattle Butler might purchase. It had been a long day and they had only gotten past Nuecestown. They could have stayed at a hotel there, but they still enjoyed camping out. Besides, it was a perfect September evening. They crossed the Nueces River on the ferry and rode just an hour longer before settling down for the night. They unpacked their bedrolls, ate dinner, and watched the sun set past the mesquite trees in the distance.

"You should look into police work. You would be ideal for it. Your imposing presence and quick hands are well suited for such work. If you like, I can call my friend Lee Hall with the Texas Rangers and see what work you can do."

"No, thank you, Mr. Butler," replied Coy as he sipped from a whiskey flask. He handed it to Butler, who tossed some back in his throat. "I like the independence I have now. I don't like to be caged like an animal. I like to be able to run free. The Red Man is right in asking why people are buying land that is just the Earth. It was here before they were and it will be here long after people are gone."

"I understand," Butler said. "But there will come a day when we will all be caged. Hopefully, we will both be gone by then."

Coy looked at Butler as if to say "you are one of the men the Red Man is speaking of," but the Coy family had also owned land before selling it to Butler. Mexicans were becoming more and more influenced by the Anglos. They were closer in looks and heritage to the Indians. The big difference was that the Indians were being forced onto reservations and told how to live, and the Mexicans were helping take over some of the Indians' old lands. The Mexicans were still considered inferior to the Anglos but were accepted by the Anglos much more than any other group. Some Mexicans with light skin and deliberate enunciation could pass as Anglos and escape persecution. All minorities were still getting persecuted despite the South's loss in the Civil War.

During Reconstruction, the government supported blacks enough to where some held public office. But that was only under military rule and did not happen again in some areas for more than 100 years. As soon as the federal agents and Carpetbaggers moved out of Texas, though, blacks lost their power. The Mexicans never received federal intervention like African Americans did, but they were able to work themselves into more power.

Mexicans were second-class citizens in San Antonio despite being in the majority. Many Anglo establishments posted signs barring Mexicans and blacks. The differences were also apparent in the brothels.

The Sporting District had three different classes of brothels. Class A was for Anglos only and was generally one dollar. Class B was for the poorer Anglos and upscale Mexicans and was 50 cents. Class C was for Mexicans and was just 25 cents.[11] Naturally, the Class A brothel was cleaner, served better drinks and was more civilized. Mexican girls worked in the Class A establishments, but Mexican men could not enter the business. Class C was operated by less desirable women of Anglo and Mexican backgrounds. Diseases were more frequent in Class C. Also, fights were more likely to break out in Class C and the whiskey was watered down.

Prostitution was illegal but mainly as a formality on the books, especially as long as it was kept in the Sporting District. Police directed men to the Sporting District and usually kept the peace around the establishments. The police were also unofficial bouncers who protected the women. Many off-duty policemen hired on with the saloons and the Sporting District businesses as bouncers. The police worked in conjunction with the women, who often told of their clients' illegal exploits. The men had a habit of bragging to the girls about robberies or stagecoach holdups. The girls, in turn, notified the police, and criminals were frequently arrested.

Florence Trent was arrested and fined $5 for being a public prostitute.[12] The *San Antonio Daily Light* of June 29, 1886, besides noting her fine, had some thoughts on her situation: "Florence Trent possesses an unusually pleasing cast of features—she looks to be young in years and in dissipation and vice, and the clearness of her complexion—the velvety smoothness of her skin, attest that she is anything but a veteran in dissipation and vice, and it is a sad pity that she cannot be snatched from a life of self-degradation, remorse and misery, and rehabilitated with respectability."[13]

Despite the public's nonchalant attitude toward prostitution, there were some brief moments of morality, mainly in the newspaper. The July 3, 1886, issue of the *San Antonio Daily Light* made these observations about Lola Flores, who was fined $5 for public drunkenness:[14] "Lola Flores is a hard case, none can be found more cheeky and reckless in the city but when Lola is loaded with whiskey, she is a Tigress. Lola is a public prostitute, which tells the entire story."[15]

The police's attitude was to let the Sporting District have their fun as long as their activity and business stayed inside the boundaries and didn't spill over into the Anglo sections. Also, as long as Mexicans and African Americans were just hurting one another, the policy was to not bother with them.

Many fruit carts were set up in front of the Alamo, but only those operated by Anglos were usually free from hassles. If the police weren't there to bother the Mexican merchants one day, most assuredly they would be back the next day. There was never anything written out about the divisiveness between the Anglos, Mexicans, and blacks. It was just expected. Richer, more prominent Mexicans were able to move in the Anglo circles and attend schools, but those were just a select few. The Coys were lucky to have the relationship with the Butlers because otherwise they would not have been as fortunate or as prosperous.

Juan Coy liked the cowboy life. He saw how the cattle drives were slowly being wiped out thanks to the expansion of the train. He reasoned that as long as the calves had to be held while being branded, cows needed feeding, and weather spooked the cattle, there would be a need for cowboys and ranch hands. Coy enjoyed working outside with the animals. It was something he learned to cherish as a child growing up in Atascosa County.

"It's a shame we're trying to get all of these people in this part of Texas," Butler told Coy one day. "The Mexicans were here long before the whites even knew about this place. Stephen F. Austin got us an invitation and he brought too many guests. Now we're advertising back East and over in Europe to come to Texas and have acres of land and plenty of cattle to raise. That's how a lot of towns got started around here—Nuecestown and New Braunfels. People bought everything they needed for a couple of hundred dollars. And yet, we're running off the people who have a legitimate right to the land."

"We did it somewhat to the Indians, too, before you ran them back even further west," Coy replied. "That drive to the West has really changed things."

"It's amazing how the railways have speeded up life so much," Butler reminisced. "On horse, it used to take almost two weeks to get across the state. The train takes just three days."

"There's nothing that can get any faster," Coy said. "It would be a miracle from God to get faster."

"Something will come along. Think of what has happened to us in the last twenty years. In less than twenty years, it will be a new century. New things are happening all of the time. When I was born, we could send messages only by mail. Now we have the telegraph. Something will happen. Yes, indeed, it will happen."

The Pony Express reached its peak twenty years earlier. Trains speeded up communications and wiped out the need for the special mail services for such long trips.

As Coy and Butler reminisced, the sun dropped totally out of view and there was not even a trace of orange, which made the sky beautiful with its tiny splashes of color. Yet it wasn't totally black with night, just a dark shade of gray which helped prepare the wolves to howl at the moon. The campfire burned brightly and the smell of coffee and burning wood filled the air.

"Mr. Butler, do you ever regret coming to Texas and leaving Mississippi behind?" Coy asked.

"Not really. To be successful in Mississippi, you had to own lots of slaves. We had a few but not a hunnert like some places did. Those people had plenty o' money. They needed it cuz the upkeep was staggering. The blacks are becoming more and more educated. Life is definitely improving for them. The Civil War was inevitable. It's sad to see so many lives lost and a nation divided over one issue, but it had to happen."

"Maybe the Mexicans can have a revolt someday to gain many of the things the blacks fought for," Juan said.

Slavery took hold because the ships from Africa in the 1700s filled a need for cheap labor in the new country. Slaves were brought over for the sole purpose of cheap labor. They were bought and sold at market just like cattle. Anglos did not treat Mexicans as equals in the labor area, but they definitely held a higher status than slaves did. Some Mexicans even owned slaves.

"One of these days, maybe we'll all be equal," Coy wished.

"Probably in a hunnert years," Butler declared. "Anyone ever involved with the Civil War and their children would have to be dead. It would have to be forgotten totally."

Chapter Eight

Pursued by the Law

Karnes County Sheriff Fate Elder rode out to Bill Young's house on a Tuesday in July 1886, just two days after Juan Coy allegedly killed a black man in Floresville. Accompanying Elder on the manhunt were Jack Bailey, Sonny Drake, and five other men. Ildefonso Coy happened to be at Young's house that day.[1]

"This Coy fellow, is he at your boss Butler's house?" Elder asked.

"I don't rightly know, sir," Ildefonso Coy said.

"Is Coy your brother?" Elder asked.

"No, he's my cousin," Coy replied. He knew that arguing with an Anglo on such a matter was useless. He also knew about the feud between the Elders and the Butlers.

"I do not know this Juan Coy. I have never heard that name before," Elder confessed.[2] "Until I started this investigation of his killing that Negro in Floresville, I'd never heard of Juan Coy. But after talking to some people, it seems that Coy is a troublemaker. The only other information I have on him is from the murder report. Hell, I don't even know what he looks like."

Ildefonso Coy continued sitting on the Youngs' front porch while Elder figured out what to do. The other men stayed on their horses. One in particular, Jack Bailey, kept his eyes on Ildefonso the entire time.

The June 29, 1886, *San Antonio Daily Light* reported that Jim Jackson, "a tough negro character," was killed at the Floresville race course by a Trevinio Coy.³ Jackson and a friend of Coy's were fighting, when Coy joined the fray. Coy and Jackson were scuffling when Coy pulled out his pistol, "placed it against the negro's neck and fired, the ball breaking the neck, killing the victim almost instantly."⁴ Coy fled on horseback that Sunday.⁵ Coy and Jackson quarreled over money at stake.⁶ There was no further word on his capture or the case.

The first name on the Coy character is different as are the victims' names, Jim Jackson and Monroe. Other details, such as the killing happening at the Floresville race course and Coy escaping on horseback, are the same.

"I want you to take these other men to William Butler's house so they can track him down," instructed Elder. "Get your horse but don't bring any firearms. I'm going to talk to Bill and get something to eat."⁷

Ildefonso Coy did as instructed, but he wasn't in a hurry to reach Butler's house. The going was slow because recent rains made the trails muddy. The grass and crops were much greener than they have been in recent times because of the rainfall.

Ildefonso had no idea where his cousin Juan was, but he didn't think he was foolish enough to stay at Butler's. Ildefonso hoped that someone who was at Young's would alert Juan if they really knew where he was. Juan was experienced enough to stay low and not even be close to family or friends more than a few days at a time. Coy never told where he hid out, but some family members suspected he stayed close to Mexico until his troubles cooled down. The lawmen close to the Mexican border were predominantly Mexican and didn't care much for Anglos and blacks. Anglos lynching a black or a Mexican north of San Antonio was frowned upon but was not a serious criminal offense. The same was true of the Mexicans harming Anglos and blacks in the valley. Coy had plenty of allies and protection in South Texas thanks to his tough reputation and his association with Butler.

Ildefonso Coy hadn't been gone long from Young's ranch when trouble started.

"I don't believe a word you said back there, Mexican," Jack Bailey declared. "I think that you're actually Juan Coy. Stop right there while I place you in handcuffs."

Everyone stopped riding. Coy looked back at Bailey and the two exchanged glances.[8]

"Jack, I hate to tell you, but the man is telling the truth," Sonny Drake said. "He's Ildefonso Coy. Juan would have whipped your ass by now. He is also taller and thinner than Juan."

"Thanks, Sonny," Coy sighed as he continued to glare at Bailey. "Can we go now?"

"Ride."

There were no more surprises on the way and there were none at Butler's house. Sheriff Elder showed up a little later and confronted Butler, accusing him of harboring a criminal. Ildefonso didn't know if Juan had been alerted to leave or if he had even been around the area, but he dared not ask anyone for fear of attracting attention.

"I'm sure if Juan killed a Negro, he was provoked or had good reason," Butler declared. "It's interesting that the sheriff of Karnes County is doing all of the work on a killing in Wilson County. Why isn't the Wilson sheriff doing anything? Why are you so interested in a Negro all of a sudden? Probably because Wilson County knows better than to waste time. Probably just because Juan is a friend and works for me. Now, get the hell off my land."

"I'll be back and you'll be in trouble. You can't control everything, Butler," Elder declared. "Saddle up, men. We'll deal with this later."

Butler and Coy stood on the porch, watching as Elder and his group rode off. A fire burned in Butler. He and Fate Elder had been enemies for a long time. Elder held the political power because of more relatives in Karnes County, but Butler held the business and monetary power. Butler's power increased even more after this confrontation, as he visited Austin to complete a big land trade.[9]

Elder's political power never translated into money, and that always bothered the sheriff. Elder tried to do anything and everything to even the financial books; this was just the latest attempt.

Butler vowed then that if their paths ever crossed again, he would rid himself of Elder for good. Elder never captured or even questioned Juan Coy for the murder in Floresville in July 1886.

Two weeks after the visit to Butler's house, Deputy Sheriff Bud Elder, Jeff Ammons, and some other men went to Ildefonso Coy's house looking for Juan Coy.[10]

The next confrontation between the two groups was just two months away.

Chapter Nine

The Daileyville Riot

Monday, September 6, 1886, was election day in Karnes County. Daileyville, which housed a store and a couple of buildings located just off the Runge Highway, was the fourth precinct in the county election, and voters were deciding on the local option of selling whiskey or not.

The Butlers were against saloons in the county, while the Elders were for it.[1] The two families were also on opposite sides on the site for Kenedy Junction, the new city planned for Karnes County. Butler also held a grudge against Fate Elder because he believed Elder, not yet sheriff then, had been involved in shooting and killing his son, Emmett.[2]

The heat was still unbearable as if it was mid-July. Too much sun and no rain in June and July continued to destroy crops. The skies finally darkened and brought rain in mid-August, but it was a hurricane that hit the South Texas coast. The hurricane wiped out the port city of Indianola. It was Indianola's second hurricane in eleven years, and this forced the remaining population to move to other cities. The hurricane's path and accompanying tornadoes tore through Gonzales, San Antonio, Luling, and New Braunfels. San Antonio suffered 85 MPH winds.[3] There was so much rain that the farmers feared an outbreak of cotton worm.[4]

The Daileyville General Store provided protection for some citizens when the shooting began that fateful day in 1886.
(Photo courtesy of Charlotte Nichols)

People milled around C. P. Dailey's store talking about the weather, crop prospects, and the cotton worm. Election day was another day to visit with friends and discuss events. The only difference between this day and the other days, when people were just standing around the general store or the barber shop, was that guns weren't allowed near the voting places on election day.

Andy Nichols, his wife and child stayed that Sunday night at the Butlers' house.[5] Also, a group of men gathered at Bill Butler's house that morning; some were finishing off breakfast and others were just in for coffee. Dr. S. G. Dailey visited Butler's house that same morning and left on horseback first. Shortly thereafter, Andy Nichols, who was married to Butler's daughter, and William Butler rode together in Nichols' wagon.[6] They headed to Daileyville.

Following Nichols and Butler were a group of Butler's workers, who converged on the election site. Among them were John Trimble, who had been boss hand for seven months; Eli Harrold;

Charles Coleman; Will Harrold; Sam Dailey; and Sykes Butler. They left William Butler's house after breakfast and went to Newton Butler's house to make plans to round up livestock. Newton talked them into voting before going to the roundup.[7]

"No guns, pistols, six-shooters or knives allowed at the election," Newton Butler instructed his men before heading to Daileyville. "Let's drop them outside the gate and we'll pick them up on the way back."[8]

Only election officials were allowed to wear guns at the polls, but somewhere, somehow enough guns wound up at the polling site and in the hands of shooters. All of Butler's men testified that there were no guns in the hack driven by Andy Nichols, just some meal sacks in the back and a blanket on the seat.[9]

Eli Harrold and Newton Butler, the last to leave Butler's house, stopped to get a bottle of whiskey before heading on. They placed their rifles with the others left earlier just inside the gate to the Butler property and rode up to catch the bigger group.[10]

Jack Pullin, Jim Pullin, and Pleas Butler were standing fifty yards in front of the store to the left of the mill road. Pleas Butler left to see Alf Taylor.[11] Most people at the scene testified as to seeing the two Mexicans ride in. Most identified Epitacio Garza and fewer recognized Juan Coy. There is talk of a black Mexican and another who was heavy-set with a long, black beard and black hair. The heavy-set Mexican with the black hair fits Coy's description, and he could have had a beard in earlier days.

Besides the sheriff and his deputies, the only guns that were obvious prior to the first shot belonged to Juan Coy and Epitacio Garza, who rode in together from the west.[12]

"Uh-oh, here comes trouble," said one of the black men whom Coy and Garza passed en route to the hack stand in front of C. P. Dailey's store. The black men—Charley Wood, Henry Philips and John Dosse—were talking to John Shuler and Moliar Mayfield. Philips recognized Garza. Mayfield asked Garza if he intended to vote, but he said he couldn't because he wasn't a citizen. Coy wasn't interested in whether he was eligible to vote or not.[13]

It was approximately 12:30 P.M. Monday, and events were already under way which would change Daileyville and area residents' lives forever.

"We had better be getting away from here," said one black man who was talking to John Shuler and Moliar Mayfield. "There is going to be some shooting here in a few minutes."[14]

Coy and Garza dismounted, hitched their horses, and pulled out their Winchester rifles. They walked to the stand with rifles in hand.

"Can we put our guns up here?" Coy asked as he and Garza stood near Nichols' hack. Both men had their Winchesters in their hands with the breach on the ground. They stood for a while, but no one ever answered them.[15]

Deputy Sheriff Jack Bailey walked out of the store and headed to the hack stand where Coy and Garza were. Bailey talked to Newton Butler near the stand.[16]

Sheriff I. L. "Fate" Elder stood near a tree a couple of hundred yards away whittling on a piece of mesquite wood. He heard loud words being exchanged and looked in that direction. Elder walked at a fast gait, continuing to whittle with the knife he had in his right hand. Finally, he tossed the wood he was whittling to the ground, tucked the knife in its sheath on his left hip, and pulled his pistol out with his right hand—all in one fluid motion.[17]

"Stop, Sheriff!" Coy called out, but the sheriff continued advancing at a fast, determined pace with his gun extended.

Eli Harrold, Will Harrold, and Sykes Butler were all leaning up against Nichols' hack just prior to the shooting.[18] The three men were between the Mexicans and the approaching Elder and would have been in the crossfire. They quickly ran to a tree where the horses were tied up to join Newton Butler and arrived just in time as the shooting commenced.[19]

"Stop!" Coy called again, but Elder didn't stop or even slow down, as he was now just ten to fifteen yards away from Coy. Elder kept his pistol leveled at Coy's head the entire march over to his target. He never said a word as he approached Coy, not even giving a warning to drop the gun.[20] Coy raised his rifle and fired a warning shot in Elder's direction. Garza fired at Elder and winged him, but Elder kept upright as Coy and Garza moved around to the end of the hack and advanced on Elder.[21] Coy shot at Elder from hip level, but Elder was lucky as the bullet hit his belt buckle.[22] Elder's luck soon ran out as Sykes Butler rushed up behind and to the right of Elder. Butler's pistol was just five inches away from the back of Fate Elder's head when he fired the gun, dropping the sheriff instantly.[23]

Another witness said Fate Elder was moving for cover behind some trees but never made it as Garza shot him in the head with his Winchester, killing him instantly.[24]

Will Harrold, who was not allowed to vote in the election, told the inquest: "Just then Fate Elder threw his right side to the Mexicans, jabbed his pistol out as though to shoot and I heard a shot. I thought it was Elder at the moment that fired. At the report, Elder made sort of a noise like 'Oh' and started to the left sideways and jabbing his pistol toward the Mexicans as if he was shooting or trying to shoot."[25]

Attorney F. R. Graves' recollection of Fate Elder's murder was closer to the account in the newspaper about being killed by a pistol. Elder had invited Graves to the election to answer a question on the procedure in arresting a person. Graves testified that a pistol's muzzle "was not more than four inches from Fate's head" when it was fired. Graves did not know or identify the assailant.[26]

"I then noticed Fate with his pistol raised rush toward the front of the hack and someone running after him pointing a pistol at the back of his head. Fate seemed to be trying to shoot someone that was on the southeast side of the hack. Just as Fate walked about half way between the two trees in front of the hack, I saw this man that was running after him put his pistol to the right back part of Fate's head and fire and the shot made Fate's hat bounce up into the air and Fate fell forward."[27]

Deputy Sheriff J. J. "Bud" Elder fired at Coy and Garza from the general store's front door. Sykes Butler, Coy, and Garza returned fire.

Sykes Butler did not have a gun before the shooting but soon found one, according to Will Harrold. "I saw him [Sykes Butler] with a shotgun when he got around behind the horses. Did not see him use it. I did not notice Eli with a gun. I did not see what Sykes did with the shotgun. I saw two Winchesters on saddles on horses, one was on Jack Bailey's saddle and the other was on a horse tied to a tree that I went around."[28]

John L. Sullivan said that he saw Sykes Butler "shooting with what looked like a six-shooter" toward the east. Sullivan said he later saw Butler throw down the pistol.[29] P. B. Butler testified that he saw Sykes with a double-barreled shotgun after the initial shots were fired.[30]

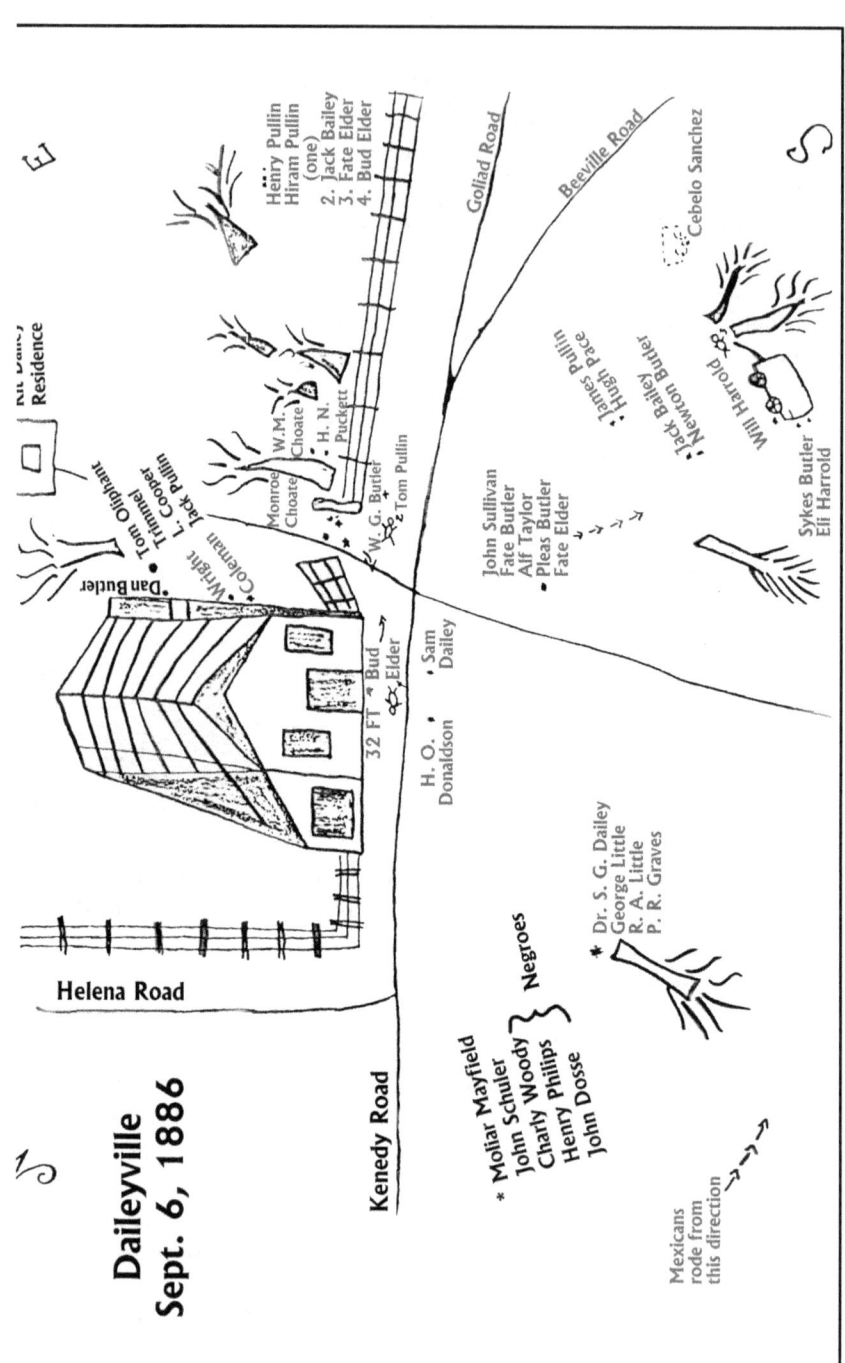

The layout of Daileyville and the participants in the election riot.

Bud Elder despised William Butler and vowed "if there was ever a showdown, he would leave the little Butlers alone and concentrate on getting the 'Old Man,'"[31] meaning William G. Butler. William Butler was by a gate near the store when the shooting started. Bud Elder fired at William Butler, who took a step or two back before he even drew his pistol.[32] Butler, never one to back away from a fight, rushed toward Elder with his pistol drawn.[33] The two men exchanged at least ten shots at close range.[34] In her autobiography, "Wofford Crossing Road," Maxine Yeater Linder reported that they approached each other "with no 'give' in either one of them—like two bulldogs."[35]

Elder was killed with bullets in each shoulder, one in his stomach and another in his ear.[36] Despite being at such close range, Butler was struck in the left ear, tearing off the tip of his earlobe.[37] Linder reported that some people claim William Butler wore some type of "steel or iron breastplate" that day. Bud Elder, who was considered a "fair shot," emptied his gun and even snapped an empty chamber into Butler's chest area but with no luck.[38]

Both men had powder burns on their faces. Elder was struck by at least six balls and two more which were little more than flesh wounds, making crevices in his skin.[39] Despite being so close to Elder, though, Butler did not fire the fatal shot. That came from the hack stand about thirty yards away from the store door. Elder was already wounded and on his knees but still trying to fire his gun. He was found with his pistol emptied but cocked and his finger still on the trigger.[40]

John Trimble rode his horse up to the live oak tree at the southeast corner of the store and hitched his horse next to others there. Trimble was talking to Tom Oliphant inside the yard when the shooting started. Trimble raced past Butler toward the gate and grabbed Monroe Choate. The two men ran around the outside of the store and into the back room.[41]

Oliphant said a shooter wore a black hat and black clothes but his head was obscured by smoke. The target was Fate Elder, who had a red beard.[42]

Jack Bailey, who was talking to Newton Butler, tried to get out of the middle of the action. He saw about twenty people shooting in what became an ambush and ran for a grove of trees near the store for protection, but was shot.[43] Estimates varied from fifty to seventy-five on the number of shots that were fired in that one-minute span.⁴⁴

Nichols pulled his uncle, Monroe Choate, to the ground just as Bailey was winged from a shot in back of him. Bailey was running with a pistol in his left hand but he dropped it when a ball tore through his left leg and left him writhing in pain.

"Don't shoot me again," Bailey cried. "I don't want to hurt anyone. I'm not part of this. Please don't shoot."

Charles Coleman testified that neither Juan Coy nor Garza shot or even attempted to shoot Bailey once he fell.⁴⁵ "They were looking over the fence where Bailey was. . . . They had their guns in their hands but did not have them in a shooting position."⁴⁶

Another ball struck Bailey in the left leg, knocking him to the ground, where he decided to stay until the shooting ended. Bailey was moved shortly thereafter to the porch at C. P. Dailey's house. Rain started falling, so Bailey was moved inside.⁴⁷ He was slipping in and out of consciousness.

"I will get well," Bailey declared, "and when I do I will kill the man that shot me."⁴⁸

Nichols and Choate ran for cover around the corner of the store and into a back room. The shooting ended shortly thereafter. They waited a few more seconds before braving a move outside to check on the conditions.

C. P. "Kit" Dailey, the store owner and the town's first postmaster, and Deputy Sheriff Vivvy Barefield, Fate Elder's brother-in-law, were both inside the store. Barefield was armed with a shotgun and was trying to fight back when Dailey ran out of the store and was accidentally hit in the foot with buckshot from Barefield's shotgun. Dailey rushed back in and jumped into a flour barrel to hide.⁴⁹

After the shooting, Dailey climbed out of the barrel only to discover himself covered with blood and flour. The wound caused him to limp the rest of his life, but it had kept him from rushing into the middle of the fracas and probably getting killed.⁵⁰

Jack Pullin, Hiram's son, was at the store that day. Henry Pullin was sitting on a box near the gate when Jack came up. Henry and Hiram Pullin had both moved to Karnes County in 1867. The Pullin and Butler families had lived in Scott County, Mississippi, in the 1840s.⁵¹

"Let me go," Jack said. "I'm ready to leave for home."

"No use to be in a hurry," Hiram Pullin replied. Hiram, fifty-eight, and his sixty-eight-year-old brother Henry continued to sit on boxes propped against the gate post.⁵² Just when the shooting started, Jack Pullin ran toward the store and inside the little room. He got inside as the shooting ceased.

"Father, what was the fighting about?" Jack asked as he turned around to his father and uncle. But his father and uncle weren't in the room.

Pullin felt a tug on his heart as he walked briskly out the store and back to the gate where he had just talked to his father and uncle a minute ago. His uncle was lying flat out on the ground, blood slowly oozing onto his shirt. The bullet wound was in Henry's chest.⁵³ Henry Pullin died instantly from the gunshot wound. Jack looked at the scene and guessed that his uncle was shot just as he was rising from the box. Jack then heard a noise not too far away. It was his father.

Hiram Pullin was lying on his side near the wheel of a hack. He was still alive but badly wounded from a ball that entered his back and went out the front.

"Son, get me a doctor," instructed Hiram Pullin. "I've been shot in the back. All I was trying to do was get out of the way. I didn't make it."

"Just rest, Father," Jack Pullin offered. "Don't talk. I'll get you help. Did you see who did it?"

"Didn't see, but I'm sure it was an accident," Hiram Pullin coughed. "How's Henry? He was right by me when the shooting started."

"Don't talk, please," Jack Pullin pleaded.

"Is he okay?" Hiram whispered.

Jack Pullin looked at his father and dropped his eyes. Hiram Pullin sobbed and coughed as he brought his right hand up to his face to wipe the tears. He opened his eyes just then and all he saw was red. The pain in his back was such that he didn't even notice he had been shot in the right wrist. The ball had entered the back of his hand and made a clean exit out the front.⁵⁴

Just then Tom Pullin, Jack's brother, ran up to the bloody scene. Tom had taken shelter behind the store when the shooting started.

"Father, are you okay?" Tom whispered. "Jack, do you need some help?"

A crowd gathers in front of the Dailey General Merchandise Store circa 1880s.
(The UT Institute of Texan Cultures at San Antonio)

"Yes, I saw some blankets in Andy Nichols' hack earlier. Go fetch me one for pa's head," instructed Henry. "See if anyone has some water, and find Doc Dailey."

Tom was gone only a couple of minutes but it seemed forever. Jack was watching Tom as he reached in the back of Nichols' hack and pulled out a blanket. The hack seemed to be at the center of all the shooting, Jack reasoned, and he wondered why someone would be riding around with blankets in the scorching September weather. When Tom pulled out the blanket, it was folded neatly. Tom jerked up a filled meal sack when he reached in to grab the blanket, but that was the only extra item in the wagon.[55]

Nichols was in the election room when the shooting started and moved into the back room after the second shot where he stayed until it was over. He said the second shot struck the wall in the election room.[56]

Grown, tough men who normally didn't flinch at a simple knife or gun wound were moaning. The smoke and smell of gunfire lingered in the air. The survivors were checking on their friends, trying to comfort them and arrange for medical care. The deputies normally would be in hot pursuit of the shooters, but there were so many people down and so many people who pulled triggers that they felt the best thing to do was take care of the wounded. Besides, the deputies knew that William Butler, Juan Coy, and Epitacio Garza were the main perpetrators of what became known as the Daileyville Riot.

Some townfolk had already come running to the bloodfest but were pulling back because of the smell and sight. They had seen shootings before, but this was closer to a slaughter. They passed the dead bodies of Sheriff Fate Elder, his brother Deputy Sheriff Bud Elder, and Henry Pullin. Hiram Pullin and Deputy Sheriff Jack Bailey were seriously wounded. County Attorney F. R. Graves, Deputy Sheriff Blair, Charles Dailey, and William G. Butler were injured but not seriously. A light rain started to fall, which washed the blood into tiny streams in front of the store.

Tom Pullin rushed back with the blanket to place under his father's head. He stroked his head and sobbed quietly. Jack applied pressure to the wound.

"Tom, it doesn't look good," Jack whispered to his brother. "I'm going to ask Andy if I can use his hack to get Mother."

Nichols loaned his hack to the Pullins and didn't get it back for "several days." He pulled the last remaining meal sack out of the hack before loaning it and dropped the sack off at the mill to get filled.[57]

Henry Pullin, who had been to the right of the store and the hack stand when the shooting started, was accidentally struck and killed instantly. His brother, Hiram Pullin, was also accidentally struck but lingered for a couple of days before dying. Hiram's wife arrived later that evening and tried to comfort her husband.

Dr. S. G. Dailey examined Jack Bailey and his leg wounds. Bailey was shot twice in the left leg and once in the right. One shot to the left leg was a flesh wound from the rear to the front, but the other broke his leg and knee joint in three places.[58] Bailey's wound to his right leg occurred when he was already on the ground and made by someone also on the ground. The ball tore through his pants between the ankle and knee and went through his thigh and into his body.[59] That would be explained by Jack Pullin's testimony of one Mexican "lying under the hack."[60]

Cebelo Sanchez told the inquest, "I was lying under a buggy just east of the hack outside. I was lying with my face down and trying to go to sleep."[61] The shooting awoke Sanchez, who eventually crawled out from under the buggy and made his way to behind a big mesquite tree. He didn't recognize the Mexicans, he said, who were firing toward the store.[62]

Bailey rested that night to recover from the shock. Dr. Graves, who had arrived at 1:00 A.M., operated on him at 9:00 A.M. The doctor suggested amputating Bailey's left leg in hopes of improving his condition.[63] Bailey drank some whiskey that morning to dull his senses before Dr. Graves operated.

"Do what ya think is best, Doc," Bailey moaned.

Bailey's wife was by his side throughout the ordeal. She asked who had shot him.[64]

"Jack Bailey made no reply but reached up his hands and pulled her down to put his mouth to her ear and whispered to her. I do not know what he said," testified Sam Dailey, a Butler employee who stayed at Butler's house Sunday night.[65]

Bailey died less than two hours after the operation without regaining consciousness.[66] Dr. Dailey said the immediate cause of death was the surgery and he "would certainly have lived several days" without the operation.[67]

Bailey had predicted something would happen between the Elders and Butlers. He told Dr. Dailey just days before that he thought William Butler did not like him but that Newton Butler and he were friends.⁶⁸

"Bill Butler isn't like Newton," Bailey said. "Newton and I went to school together and we've been friends. The Butlers and Elders can't stand each other. I'm surprised nothing has happened 'tween them two yet. Since the Elders have the power here, they are so mean to the Butlers that the Butlers are going to have to fight them."

An inquest was formed at the request of the Karnes County attorney. The inquest's ruling was signed September 13, 1886, and appeared September 16 in the *San Antonio Daily Express*.⁶⁹ It stated in part:

"We, the jury empanelled and sworn to inquire into the cause, manner, etc. of the death of I. L. Elder, Bud Elder and Henry Pullin, find that Henry Pullin came to his death by a gun shot fired by some one, striking him accidentally; that I. L. Elder came to his death by gun and pistol shot wounds, fired by Epitacio Garza and John or Juan Coy and Sykes Butler; that Bud Elder came to his death by gun or pistol shot wounds inflicted by a gun or pistol fired by Wm. G. Butler."⁷⁰

It was signed by the jury members of Precinct No. 1 in Karnes County, including D. B. Butler, justice of the peace. The jury concluded: "And so ends another episode of crime in our county, in which the officers of the law and conservators of the peace are foully dispatched. When will such things cease?"⁷¹

There were more fireworks to come from the election day shootout.

CHAPTER TEN

The Sensation of the Day

The repercussions from what became known as the Daileyville Riot or the Butler-Elder Feud almost grew into an international incident. It certainly was the focus of South Texas talk for a number of years.

All of Butler's men testified at the inquest that they only went to Daileyville to vote on the local option and were totally surprised by the shooting. They said that William Butler didn't tell them of any such activity planned that day. They also testified that Coy and Garza were not under Butler's employ at that time and they hadn't even seen Coy immediately prior to the shooting.[1] The last time Will Harrold said he saw Coy was "on Tuesday or Wednesday after he killed the negro in Wilson County on Sunday. I saw him at the Rosser tank watering his horse. . . . The last time I ever saw Garcia [Garza] before the Daileyville killing was the time at the Floresville District Court when his case there was dismissed."[2] There is no mention of the charge.

John Trimble stated: "I did not go to Daileyville to fight. I went to vote for local option and I voted for it. I know nothing of any conspiracy by Mr. W. G. Butler and others to fight there that day. I am satisfied there was no such conspiracy. It could not have been without my knowing it. Mr. Butler always told us to keep out of difficulties."[3]

Graves, county attorney, wired Governor John Ireland seeking four Texas Rangers to help in arresting Coy, Garza, and the others involved in what the *San Antonio Daily Express* was calling a riot.[4] Coy, who was already wanted for a murder in Floresville, rode off swearing he would never be captured.

Graves was present that day to render an opinion on arrest papers Fate Elder had for someone. Graves said if the unnamed person voted, Elder couldn't arrest him unless it was for a felony. If the man didn't go to vote, Elder could arrest him.[5]

"I did not at any time hear him mention that he thought there would be any trouble there," Graves told the inquest of his dicussions with Elder.[6]

Butler had rid himself of his two major nemeses—Fate and Bud Elder. He regretted the deaths of the two elderly Pullin men. Butler was struck in the shootout, the first time he had been shot. Bud Elder shot him in the earlobe when the two were firing at close range.

A possible motive for Butler was retaliation for the way Elder treated him. Bailey had said that the Elders "were so abusive toward them [the Butlers] that a fight would be the result of it."[7] Another motive was a civil suit Fate Elder had urged a citizen to file against Newton Butler. Newton Butler allegedly hit a man in a Kenedy restaurant, and Elder persuaded the man to file a civil suit. William Butler got wind of the suit and made some accusations against Elder. Elder promised Graves that he would not confront or even discuss the situation with Butler if he was at the election.[8]

William G. Butler testified that the only person he saw shooting a gun was Bud Elder, and he saw several with guns after the shooting but did not recognize them.[9] Butler testified: "I did not see Epitacio Garcia [Garza] for a day or two before the shooting. He did not tell me he would be there. . . . I did not notice whether he had a gun or pistol. . . . The Mexican that was with E. Garcia [Garza], I think was John Coy . . ."[10]

Governor Ireland sent some Texas Rangers to investigate, but the usual closed society did not divulge anything that could be used for evidence or even speculation. They asked questions around town and the entire county but left knowing nothing more than when they arrived. The only story the Rangers received from the Butler side was how the lawmen instigated the fight. William Butler and Ranger Captain Lee Hall started cementing their relationship during this time.

Juan Coy and Epitacio Garza rode off without even the slightest scrape. No one gave chase. They stayed near the battle site for two hours and no one made a move to arrest them.[11]

Coy and Garza showed up at Jesse Perez' ranch one day before sunup to see Perez. The men explained that they were in a hurry for a trip to Mexico and wanted their horses shod as soon as possible. Coy told his cousin about the whiskey election and the subsequent shooting.[12]

Perez quickly shod the horses, but the sense of urgency was false as Coy and Garza stayed an extra four days before heading south.[13]

The killings shocked area residents and people in San Antonio, mainly because of William G. Butler's status in Karnes County and South Texas. The incident surprised those who didn't know of the bad blood between the Elders and the Butlers.

The *Victoria Advocate* reported in the September 18, 1886, issue that the shooting was just a continuation of the feud which had been brewing for years. "A few days ago, since the recent bloody affray, a man named Miller, who lives at Helena, was met by an adherrent of the Butler faction and notified that in case he considered his life 'worth a d—n,' he had better leave the county. Considering the character of the messenger, Miller at once proceeded to do as requested."[14]

Lieutenant Rudd, formerly with the state police, was appointed sheriff of Karnes County. Governor Ireland sent a group of Rangers to Karnes County to help maintain order.[15]

The lawlessness of the entire situation also shocked people and brought some reaction.

One anonymous San Antonio lawyer suggested in the September 17, 1886, issue of the *San Antonio Daily Express* that Karnes County be sliced up and distributed to surrounding counties. "He says it is no doubt the most lawless and benighted county in the state, so much so that any officer who attempts to do his duty without fear or favor runs the risk of being shot down at any moment. To arrest the perpetrators does no good. By attaching Karnes to some other county, the trials would all be had in the county to which it is attached with much more certainty of justice to all parties."[16]

It didn't take long for a reaction to the charges of lawlessness to appear in the *San Antonio Daily Express*. Thomas Ruckman, founder of nearby Helena, had his letter published on September 22, 1886. He said the previous letter gave the "wrong impression" and that a few bad people were bringing a bad reputation on the entire county. "Many of us have had our holmes [sic] here since the organization of the county—comfortably fixed and expect to live and die here, and we don't wish our friends in other parts of the world to think that we live among, or are a community of savages, roughs and cutthroats. I will challenge any one to point out any county that has any better people than the mass of our citizens, who are no more responsible for the crimes committed among us, than any other county is for its crime."[17]

Ruckman took to task the "prominent San Antonio lawyer" who suggested that the "lawlessness county" be carved up and distributed to neighboring counties. Ruckman reminded readers about Austin City Marshal Ben Thompson, who was shot down in San Antonio, "which all of the prominent lawyers in San Antonio could not prevent." The lawyer should check out the number of crimes in San Antonio before criticizing events in Karnes County, Ruckman added.[18]

Ruckman recalled some of the past killings in the county and explained how swift justice was dealt. The first case he mentioned was Sheriff Leary's murder at the hand of Emmett Butler. The second example was a Dr. Trader, who killed an innocent young man who went to the doctor's house for treatment of an injured hand. Trader, who was drunk when he shot the boy, was immediately arrested, placed in jail, indicted, convicted, and sentenced to five years in prison. "Now he is out under bond, and likely never will be punished. Our citizens expressed great indignation that such a crime should go unpunished, but Karnes county is not responsible for a DeWitt county jury's verdict, let it be right or wrong."[19]

Ruckman recounted some of the events surrounding the Daileyville Riot. He said Coy was an escaped criminal from Wilson County and that Garza had been indicted by Karnes County, but a Wilson County jury found him not guilty. "Are our people held accountable for these two Mexicans suddenly appearing on the ground at Daileyville that unfortunate day, opening fire on the sheriff and shooting recklessly into a crowd of harmless and unarmed men, and bringing to a crisis a feud that had been growing for years between two families, increasing in hatred and vindictiveness as it grew older, aggravated by talk and threats on both sides until it culminated in a fatal combat and the killing of innocent and uninterested parties? . . . . My principle object is to let the world know that our county is not filled with man-eaters and that it is not dangerous to come among us."[20]

As expected, Coy and Garza headed south to Mexico after the shootings. Garza went deep into the interior, to Mexico City, but Coy stayed in Nuevo Laredo.[21] Coy went from bar to bar, drinking his way around the town and even engaging in a couple of fights. His habits were known, or else someone talked, because the police knew right where to look. Bexar County Deputy Sheriff Mariano Garcia rode down to Nuevo Laredo and kept an eye on Coy.[22] Garcia waited until Coy got drunk and passed out, placed him in a hack with some women, and took him across the river. As soon as they were on Texas soil, Garcia arrested Coy and placed him in the Webb County Jail.[23]

Just five weeks after the shooting, Coy had been captured in Mexico on October 10, 1886. State Ranger Capt. George H. Smith, Webb County Sheriff Dario Sanchez, and Garcia then turned Coy over to Karnes County Sheriff L. W. Rudd, who left for Karnes County on October 11.[24] Perez offered a slightly different account, stating in his diary that Garcia took Coy to San Antonio[25] as opposed to the newspaper's version of Rudd taking Coy to Karnes City.[26]

The October 12 story in the *San Antonio Daily Express* stated that the *Mutualista*, the Mexican federal police, claimed Coy's arrest was illegal.[27]

"There is said to have been a good deal of excitement over the arrest at Nuevo Laredo, Mexico, the *Mutualista* claiming it was done without due process of law, and alleges that Mexico has good grounds for declaring war against the United States," reported the *Daily Express*. "The officers, however, say they had a requisition from the governor, and that the arrest was legally effected."[28]

Charges of murder, unlawfully carrying a pistol, and assault were filed in Karnes County against Daniel Butler and Garza on October 14, 1886.[29]

The first court appearance for Coy was in Karnes City on

October 16, 1886. The court decided that the Wilson and Karnes county jails were insecure and that Coy should be kept in Bexar County until time for trial.[30]

Coy received a change of venue from Karnes to Wilson County. "He will consequently be tried at Floresville for the murders at Daileyville some weeks ago, if not for the murder of the negro at Lodi."[31] The *Express* reported on October 20 that Coy had already been charged with "half a dozen or more murders" and had already served one prison term.[32]

The next day's *Express* included Butler's status with the court. Evidence from the jury of inquest was submitted. William G. Butler, indicted for the murder of Deputy Sheriff Bud Elder, was placed under $10,000 bond, which was secured by P. B. Butler, John Rutledge, and J. D. Newberry.[33] Eli Harrold, charged with killing Sheriff Fate Elder, posted $2,500 bond by W. G. Butler, N. G. Reynolds, and A. J. Jordan.[34] No bond was set for Coy, who was indicted for killing Fayette Elder and complicity in killing Sheriff Bud Elder. Coy was also under indictment for a murder that occurred in Wilson County in July 1886.[35]

Sykes Butler was arrested for killing Sheriff Fate Elder and posted a $5,000 bond from W. G. Butler, M. L. Butler, and P. B. Butler. There was another indictment against Sykes Butler for murder in the first degree with a $15,000 bond, which was posted by the same three men.[36]

The Karnes County Court also granted a change of venue in the Coy and Butler cases to Wilson County. The article said the prosecution would attempt to prove conspiracy, while Butler's side would argue self-defense.[37]

"The outcome will be watched with great interest as the Daileyville affair was one of the bloodiest affrays recorded in the wild history of the state," according to the *Daily Express*. "Joined to the exceptionally sensational features of the affair is the large wealth of William Butler, the principal defendant who is one of the richest and best known pasture men in that section of country."[38]

The fall and winter terms for Wilson County court opened Tuesday, November 30, 1886, according to the December 1, 1886, *San Antonio Daily Express*, and it was reported that the Butler and Coy cases were scheduled for Monday, December 6. Coy was a prisoner under Sheriff Rudd's care, and Butler was out on bond. Several

Texas Rangers, Adjutant General W. H. King, and several visiting lawyers were also seen around town and in court awaiting the trial.[39]

The *Express* of December 8 reported that the cases involving Butler, Coy, and others connected with the Daileyville Riot were continued until the next court term.[40]

The problems over Coy's arrest continued to fester as more charges were levied. A story in the December 14, 1886, issue of the *San Antonio Daily Express* reported that Nuevo Laredo authorities noted some irregularities in Coy's extradition from Mexico to the United States: "... he was crossed over to Texas in the wee, small hours of the night, and that the chief of police received part of the reward for his assistance. The receiving of rewards by Mexican officials is something unknown, and strictly prohibited; consequently the chief of police finds himself in hot water, as the federal judge has ordered an inquiry to be made. Pedro Morales, the chief of police, and several policemen and the jailer have been arrested and placed in jail by order of the federal judge, and the jail placed under guard of federal soldiers."[41]

Unfortunately, news from Mexico was reported very sporadically in San Antonio and no follow-up story was found.

A story in the December 12, 1886, *San Antonio Daily Express* summed up the case to that point. The writer started with the condition of Karnes County, describing how it was ripe for murder. "It is brushy, broken and a large part of it, uninhabitable. It was the starting place of the Taylor feud which has passed into history. Its latest sensation was what has come to be known as the 'Butler Killing' or 'the Daileyville Riot.'"[42]

The *Daily Express* article continued, sometimes in a flashy sense: "When it [the shooting] was finished there were enough dead men on the ground to stock an amateur graveyard and the rest were carted off, wounded and spent, to die another time. It was the sensation of the day. People who read the newspapers expected an immediately subsequent lynching. That which has taken place illustrates the law's delay."[43]

The *Express* article said that Butler's cattle "roam on a thousand hills and his acres as well nigh measureless." Butler, one of Karnes County's wealthiest men, enjoyed his wealth and privacy. His word was bond and "his instinct of self-preservation a good deal better than either." He was indicted and posted bond. Butler was also described as one of the principal participants in the riot, according to the newspaper. His chief associate was Juan Coy, who was described as "a noted Mexican desperado." Coy was said to be in hiding for a murder he committed near Floresville.[44]

The entire incident from the shooting to the arrest to the trial drew considerable attention. "There was a big flourish made over the cases. Distinguished San Antonio counsel were employed. A battle of legal weapons was looked for. Last Monday the cases came up for trial. They were continued. Other participants, above and beyond William Butler and Juan Coy, were indicted. They have never been arrested."[45]

The widows of both Bud and Fate Elder and Jack Bailey filed civil suits against William G. Butler, but all three were dismissed on October 9, 1888, in Karnes County.[46]

William Harrold was found guilty on April 15, 1887, in Karnes County for carrying a sidearm within half a mile from a polling place. He was fined $100 and costs and would be jailed until the amount was paid. Harrold appealed and posted a $300 surety bond.[47]

Sykes Butler pleaded not guilty, posted a $15,000 bond, and received a change of venue from the Karnes County court on April 16, 1887. It was declared that a "dangerous combination against him instigated by influential persons" would prohibit him from receiving a fair trial. The case was set for the first Monday in June 1887. A jury on April 21, 1887, found Sykes Butler not guilty of carrying a gun within half a mile of a voting place on election day.[48]

William G. Butler pleaded not guilty to the charge of unlawfully carrying a firearm within half a mile from a voting place. The jury, led by foreman W. L. More, found Butler guilty on April 19, 1887, and fined him $100. Butler filed to set the verdict and judgment aside and asked for a new trial, but was denied on all counts. He immediately appealed, but no records were discovered of any decisions on the appeals. P. B. Butler and J. D. Newberry posted a surety bond of $300 for William G. Butler. Newberry was justice of the peace, Precinct 4, for Karnes County, and P. B. Butler was related to D. B. Butler, who was justice of the peace, Precinct 1.[49]

A lack of witnesses led a grand jury to clear the Butlers, according to Maxine Yeater Linder's autobiography. William Butler was released as the grand jury decided Bud Elder had fired on him first.[50]

William G. Butler pleaded guilty to aggravated assault on April

21, 1887, and was fined $25 and costs.[51] Eli Harrold was freed that same day after a hung jury failed to decide on his murder case after just a day of deliberations.[52]

Fees in Sykes Butler's case ran up to $24.30, with $9 for summoning eighteen witnesses and $8.00 for attending prison under a writ of habeas corpus. Another case against Sykes Butler cost the county $16 in paperwork.[53]

The courts in small counties usually met just three or four times a year for about a month each. Once a case was continued it was usually at least two more months before the opportunity even arose again. Juan Coy's time in court came during the June 1887 session in Wilson County. After dispensing with the civil docket, Judge McCormick moved to the criminal docket on Monday, June 13, 1887. Jury selection took most of that Monday but the trial moved into opening statements by late Monday evening, according to the *San Antonio Daily Express* on June 15.[54]

Normally, cases had one prosecuting attorney and one defense attorney—two on each side at the most. The Coy case had seven lawyers on each side. Prosecuting the case were District Attorney T. H. Spooner, W. H. Burges, A. Jack Evans, A. R. Stevenson, F. R. Graves, T. W. Hankinson, and James Wilson. Defense lawyers were T. T. Teel, L. H. Brown, L. S. Lawhon, E. R. Lane, J. B. Polley, T. P. Morris, and C. H. Mayfield.[55]

Seven lawyers hired by Butler were sitting on Coy's side in the trial. Coy's fate before the judge and jury would be a good indicator of Butler's own case.

The Coy trial not only brought out defense lawyers but also plenty of spectators and some rain, which started Monday afternoon and continued off and on. There were extra law enforcement personnel just in case there was any uprising by the Coy or Butler camps. The excitement also kept the town sober as the newspaper writer reported not seeing any drunks in town since court opened for the trial. "The town is full of people, a great many of them having come from Karnes County," the paper described.[56]

"Farmers detained in town on the jury are kicking about being kept away from their growing crops."[57] On Saturday, June 18, 1887, the *San Antonio Daily Express* reported that the Juan Coy case was still being argued. Testimony was still being heard. "The witnesses in this case will probably be the same as in the Butler case, yet to be tried."[58]

Butler's camp trotted up plenty of witnesses, claiming they had no idea how all of the guns instantly materialized that fateful day in September. The defense pointed out that Coy was an officer of the law and could legally have a gun despite the election day code that prohibited guns near a polling site.

The grand jury condemned the old jail and said that the commissioner's court will "probably advertise for bids" for a new jail since the old jail was full and overflowing.[59]

The commissioners did award a contract to build a $14,000 jail to B. L. Reid, a Calaveras brick maker.[60]

Family and friends of William Butler packed the courthouse and responded vocally to the proceedings. The prosecution called Butler to the stand but was unsuccessful in getting him to implicate Coy or Garza in initiating the action that fateful day. Instead, Butler told how the sheriff and his deputies overreacted and drew their guns first.

"He did what any normal person would do who had a gun coming straight toward their head," Butler stated. "He protected himself."

The trial lasted more than a week, finally concluding on Tuesday, June 21, as reported in the *Daily Express* on June 22. The case ended in a hung jury, which was not unexpected.

"The Juan Coy murder case was given to the jury last Saturday evening, the attorneys having argued through the entire day. It was said when the jury was first sworn that they never would agree and they did not. Monday night one of the jurymen, A. V. Smith, became suddenly and violently insane, and doctors were sent for. He seemed to imagine other members of the jury wanted to kill him. The district judge could do nothing but discharge the jury. They were about equally divided, standing six for acquittal and six for conviction for murder in the second degree. The case will be sent to another county."[61]

Karnes County was charged $7.00 in court costs for the Juan Coy murder case in April. Included in the $7.00 bill were 10 cents for entering the indictment, filing five papers at 10 cents each for 50 cents, 25 cents for docketing cause, and 75 cents for making a transcript of change of venue of 750 words at 10 cents for every 100 words. Court costs for Eli Harrold's change of venue hearing in his murder charge was $10.05. His transcript was 600 more words and there were two judgments made. In Sykes Butler's murder case, M. O'Neal received $4.80 in expenses from the county, three cents a mile for sixty miles and $1 a day for three days of lodging.[62]

It is doubtful the Coy case, and certainly the Butler case, ever made it to another county to be tried. Research in other neighboring counties provided no clues. Newspaper records for Karnes and Wilson counties do not date back that far, and there was nothing discovered in the San Antonio newspapers for that period.

The only mention of Coy serving any prison time was the murder case for which he served five years (from 1879 to 1884). There was never any indication that William G. Butler served any time in prison for any type of offense. He was probably granted a continuance that the prosecution conveniently forgot about. He may have struck a deal with the district attorney's office that the case would stay in the continuance category forever unless he got into more trouble. Today, these types of cases resemble deferred adjudication.

Daileyville started in 1869 as a general store.[63] The town had a population of twenty-five, but it soon died after the Shoot-Out.

County officials were still debating on where to locate the new town of Kenedy Junction. The Shoot-Out changed the original location, according to Linder in "Wofford Crossing Road," because one of the men killed in the Shoot-Out owned property that had been chosen for the new city along the railroad.[64]

One man's death left title to the widow and minor children with legal complications, according to "Wofford Crossing Road." Because of the legal problems, the storm's destruction and the junction of the branch railway line to Houston being several miles south of Daileyville, the new townsite was moved to its present location. The city was named in honor of Captain Kenedy, who saved the railroad and made the new town possible.[65]

The town was originally called Kenedy Junction, but it was officially changed June 21, 1887, to Kenedy.[66] Some people referred to the town as "Six-Shooter Junction," as evidenced by letters addressed as late as the 1940s.[67]

Coy was the test case for Butler, and both survived the legal system. The Daileyville Riot was the only incident discovered on the books which directly involved Butler in a criminal case. It was just another in a long line for Coy, though.

CHAPTER ELEVEN

Family Life

Juan Coy was approximately twenty-five years old when he married Manuela Rios in Floresville on May 28, 1867. Father Godard performed the ceremony. Jesus Garcia and Cleta Saila signed as witnesses.[1]

The San Antonio Archdiocese records show a baptism record for Manuela Rios on July 7, 1849, exactly one month after her birth. Her parents are listed as Mateo Rios and Lenora Marquis. Manuela's godparents were Talamantes and Rosa de la Garza. Father Calvo baptized Manuela at San Fernando Cathedral.[2]

Juan Coy and Manuela Rios had four children: Victoriano, born in 1869; Antonio; Juan, born July 18, 1875[3]; and Alejos, who died while in his teens.

Family ties have traditionally been strong in the Mexican lifestyle, and Juan Coy's family was no exception. Unfortunately, Coy's imprisonment forced Manuela to leave her husband while he was in prison. Victoriano was fifteen years old by the time his father was released from prison. The four children stayed with the Perez and Butler families when their mother left.

Coy was like a caged animal, especially after the divorce from Manuela. He was bitter that she didn't stay around. It is not known whether the prison term was the reason that she divorced Juan.

Coy promised Butler he would cut back his drinking, but that didn't last long. He had been back home in Floresville just days when the urge to drink hit him again. With that came the next step of fighting. His fighting prowess was considerably improved, thanks to his time in jail.

Not all of his time was spent in saloons or on the Butler farm. He took the children on some outings but couldn't handle the day-to-day activities. He did find time to take his children to church, which led to romance.

Coy met Jacoba Reyes, who was just fourteen years old, at church. His time in prison had toughened him, but also in a way calmed him down. She became his second wife less than a year after their meeting at church. He was blunt about needing a mate for himself and a mother for Juan and Alejos (Victoriano and Antonio were already out on their own). She wanted to get out of her house and start her own family. She was thirty years younger than him, and the families were old friends. Juan's cousin, Ildefonso Coy, had been baptized on March 17, 1850, and his godparents were Yldefonso Leal and Jacoba Travieso, Jacoba's mother.[4]

The relationship between Juan Coy and Jacoba Reyes started simply with casual talk. It grew over the next several months until they married on July 23, 1890, in Wilson County by Rev. E. Y. Seale.[5]

Coy decided he wanted to marry after going through the ordeal of accompanying Butler to Helena to retrieve Emmett Butler's body. Watching and talking to Butler on that long, sorrowful trip made Juan realize he needed a wife to complete his family. He was not the fatherly type like Butler, so the nurturing had to come from a mother.

It was common for the woman to consent to marriage despite having less than loving feelings for the man. A woman's family, especially the mother, always felt she could learn to love the man. After all, that's what she did with her husband. Jacoba Reyes liked the fact that Juan was strong and independent. He would be a good protector and an adequate provider because of his relationship with Butler. She later realized that Juan had no property, that Butler owned the land and house. Her grandparents owned one of the largest ranches in south Bexar County, Las Mulas.

Butler gave Juan the land and the house his family had resided on for years, but there were no formal legal papers stipulating such.

Juan and Jacoba Coy, his second wife. She was approximately thirty-three years younger than Juan.
(Photo courtesy of Edward Coy Ybarra)

Coy and Butler trusted each other and understood the arrangement.

The wedding was small and simple. They received their marriage license two days prior at the courthouse in Floresville. The Butlers gave the Coys a horse and a cow as wedding presents. The Butlers helped Jacoba move into her new house later that afternoon. Jacoba, born September 20, 1874,[6] was just fifteen years old when she married the forty-eight-year-old Juan Coy. Victoriano, Juan's oldest son from his first marriage, was five years older than his new stepmother.

Coy enjoyed spending time with his two younger sons as they often went hunting, fishing, or riding horses. The three were out hunting prairie dogs one day when Alejos spotted one and gave chase. Alejos climbed over a fence but lost his footing and the gun accidentally discharged, striking him in the chest.

Alejos, who had just entered his teenage years, suffered for a short time in the field before taking his last breath. Juan, who was covered with his son's blood, carried the lifeless body back to the house.

The loss was devastating for the family, but especially for Juan. He was just now enjoying the life of a father after being on the run, at work, or in prison through most of their childhood. Juan felt this was God's punishment for the people he had killed in the past, and he withdrew from everything for weeks.

"Dad, it's not your fault," Juan Junior told his father. "You've got to stop blaming yourself. It could have happened to anyone. Alejos just made a mistake."

"I know, son, I know," the elder Coy replied. "It's just the pain of losing someone that you created. I never realized how sudden and dramatic all of it was."

The death forced Juan to stop and reevaluate the life he had led. He was a hired gun, having killed at least thirty people.

Juan stayed around the house for a long time, not venturing out for any law enforcement work or work for Butler. He wanted another son by the same name. Jacoba became pregnant with Coy's fifth child weeks after they married.

Mrs. Butler counseled Jacoba on what to expect in the childbearing stages. Juan consoled his wife and expressed confidence that she could handle it. Alejos, the only child of Juan and Jacoba Coy, was born April 27, 1891.[7] His mother was just sixteen years old. Coy's three older children were already grown and out of the house.

Jacoba hoped that another child would keep Coy at home more. He told her that he stayed home much less with his first wife. Jacoba said she wasn't the first wife and wanted him home more. Soon he was working more and more for Butler and as a deputy sheriff, which sometimes took him out of town. Even when he was in town, he made up stories that required him to be at some saloon. He wasn't drinking like before, but he wanted an escape to forget Alejos' death. The birth of the second Alejos did help to keep him at home much more.

Jacoba was a good cook, fixing the usual Mexican staple of beans, rice, tortillas, and meat. When Juan wandered the countryside, he practiced his aim by hunting rabbits. It was not unusual for him to bring home a few rabbits from just a casual horse ride. He brought home the rabbits, skinned them, and presented Jacoba with that night's meat. What he didn't eat that day he salted and saved for the next day or two. If he brought home more than a week's worth of food, he skinned the hares and gave some to the Butlers or other area families. Families around the Honey took care of each other with food and pelts.

The hides were combined to make some warm jackets and blankets for the Coy family and for trading for other household items. Juan taught the children at a young age to use a knife and how to kill and skin rabbits and deer. He taught both of his wives to hunt, and they adapted quickly to the gun.

"It's good to see you use the gun for something useful and not just for killing," Jacoba said. Juan had told her the entire story about his job and how many men he had killed.

Jacoba wanted Juan to take her out more. She suggested a trip to San Antonio to the Turner Opera House. She had met Jacobo's family, who offered room in their house if they ever visited San Antonio. But Juan still said no. Jacoba was pregnant in late 1890 when Juan finally took his wife and Juan Junior to San Antonio. The pregnancy did not dampen her enthusiasm.

Floresville was only thirty miles from San Antonio, but it was almost a full day's journey, especially with one child and a pregnant woman. The family set out one Saturday morning early in the fall and arrived late in the afternoon. They stayed overnight at the park and left the next morning in time to get back home before nightfall.

The trip to San Antonio was an experience for everyone. They visited the San Fernando Cathedral and marveled at its spectacular design and stained glass windows. The Alamo was run-down and the area in front overrun with chili queens and vendors. Nearby was the Menger Hotel, which offered some of the finest hotel rooms in the country for $2. The San Antonio River was just a block away, but the smell of dumping area hung in the air. People's shacks backed up to the river, and no one thought anything about emptying their trash in the river. The river had become swampy in some places and downright smelly in all areas near downtown. Mosquitoes bred constantly in the area. Some of the plants that covered the banks of the river looked black from disease but were actually just covered with mosquitoes.

The flies from the river area mixed in with the flies from the streets as they hovered over horse manure. The horse manure stayed where it landed and either became dusty when the sun beat down on it or turned into mud pies from the rain. Either way, it smelled and it attracted flies. The smell of horse manure was quite common as it naturally seeped into the clothes and was blown into the houses.

Juan avoided the Sporting District near Commerce and Dolorosa streets for fear of being spotted by some of his drinking buddies, the police or, worse, his enemies.

They had just left the San Fernando Cathedral and were walking across the street toward the Main Plaza when Juan saw someone he thought he recognized. The man was coming out of the Bexar County Courthouse with its splendid red brick facade. Because Juan had been in so many fights through the years, he always had to look over his shoulder. Coy glanced at the man but still couldn't place his face. It didn't matter who or where; Juan didn't want to spark a memory in the man before he could remember himself.

Jacoba was already walking close to Juan, but he pulled her a little closer. Jacoba didn't suspect a thing and neither did Junior. The man kept getting closer so Juan kept getting closer, to his wife. Surely such a family man wouldn't be mistaken for an almost lone wolf fighter and killer. The man passed without incident and Juan breathed a sigh of relief.

That was the bad part about being a hired gun. You couldn't go anywhere with your family and expect to have a quiet time. You were always cautious because that type of person didn't have typical hours, boundaries, or rules. Anything went—anytime, anywhere.

Coy took his family close to Government Hill to look at the Quadrangle where the U.S. Army once held Chief Geronimo. He felt a kinship toward Geronimo because both were facing changing lifestyles and having a hard time keeping in step with the new world. Jacoba wanted to see President Harrison, but Juan reminded her that he had come for a couple of days in April but wasn't able to ride in the parade because of all the rain. She thought that he was staying in town for the summer.

When they returned home to Floresville, Juan told his wife about his fear in San Antonio. She understood the fear but tried to talk Juan into changing his ways.

"If you change and people notice, they will forgive you," she explained.

"No, it is a burden I will bear for the remainder of my life," Coy said. "Revenge is the only answer for those ways, and I must always be on watch. The only forgiving people will do is when I am dead."

Butler questioned Coy on his sanity when the boss heard afterwards that Coy had gone to San Antonio. Butler had warned Coy to always be careful, and going to San Antonio was just foolish.

"Juan, you can get yourself killed up there," Butler said. "There are enough people who want both of us dead without you going there so they can pin targets on our backs."

"Dammit, Bill, things are just getting too crowded for me," Coy reacted. "I like the freedom of the trail. The open range. I miss all of the cattle drives. We had a purpose back then, Bill. We don't do anything now."

"I know, my friend," Butler said. "Things have indeed changed, and that's why we have to be more careful. The police and rangers are serious now. You can't buy off police or judges to look the other way when something goes wrong like the old days."

The two walked along a dirt trail toward Butler's house. The trail started out as a simple dirt road but soon became the main road to the railroad stop. A small cabin was near the main house for when Coy and other cowboys stayed at the ranch for work. It had housed a large group of men back in the cattle drive days. The windows were the latest addition, with neatly built wooden frames holding them in place. Jacoba had sewn together beautiful calico drapes for the windows. Two dogs tried to catch a breeze on the shady side of the house but with little luck.

"If it doesn't rain soon, we'll have hell to pay with the crops," Coy said. "The wheat is almost shriveled dead and the cattle have almost drained the stock pond dry. I hear Wiatrek down the road has already lost some cows because of the heat."

"We're all suffering," Butler lamented. "We made a pact last month to share resources and we have been. But it's still killing all of us. This is the worst I've seen it in the thirty years I've been here."

"*Sí*, my family has mentioned some other time in the '30s or '40s but there was nothing here to begin with. It was before the white man took over."

"I came here almost forty years ago and it seems as if I never lived in Mississippi. I never want to go back there. This state has provided me with so much."

"You have grown to be a powerful man, Mr. Butler," Coy said. "You have all of the railroad line. Public officials seek your advice, and you own all of this land and cattle."

"True, but just owning cattle one day will not mean that much. Nor will being a farmer. More and more people are moving to Texas for different reasons, and they will need land. The public officials will find a way to give them my land. You know why? Because the United States does not want to become like England was years ago and have land barons with their fiefs. They have already demonstrated that by the 15th Amendment, which gave blacks the right to vote. They are trying to equalize many things."

"I appreciate that you allowed me to claim that I had land so I could vote in the elections."

The two men continued walking while chatting about current events. They heard something in the brush and stopped to check the intruder. Coy spotted the rattlesnake first and quickly whipped his pistol out of his holster and shot the snake—all in one fluid motion. The force of the bullet striking the snake's head into the sand propelled the snake into the air tail first. Coy walked over, kicked it to make sure it was dead, picked it up, and slung it over his shoulder.

"Tonight's dinner," Coy proclaimed. Butler smiled at his friend. The two had been through so much together. Coy had remained the same while Butler gained wealth, power, and fame—sometimes thanks to Coy's activities.

Rain finally started falling days later and brought some relief, but the rainfall was far behind schedule for the year. The stock ponds filled and some grass was able to grow. Pecan farmers near Seguin had a poor season because of the drought as did the cotton farmers further south. Some area farmers were experimenting with fruits that seemed to tolerate the heat. Their big test would be later in the winter with the freezes. Butler was going to keep an eye on that.

With the rains also came the time for the children to begin school again. The school was just one room, and the teacher covered the first eight grades. Juan Junior wasn't happy about it and begged his new mother to allow him to work with his father in the fields or with the cattle.

"You've got to learn how to read," said Juan Coy, who could only make his mark. "I want you to be able to read and do your numbers. Victoriano and Antonio know their numbers and can write their name."

"But some of the kids at the white school make fun of me."

"Just ignore them. You are an American as much as they are! You tell them that."

"Why are we Americans but not Mexicans, and why do we go to the Mexican school?" Juan Junior asked.

"We were born in America but we're of Mexican descent. My father was a Mexican because there was no America here when he was born. He became a Texan later when it became independent and then he became an American when Texas became a state in the United States. Those kids' grandfathers were the same way. Their grandfather was a foreigner because this was part of Mexico before it became part of America. The Mexicans, whites, and blacks each have their own school. Sometimes, they'll put the Mexicans and whites together."

Coy felt strongly about his being an American and equally strong about being of Mexican ancestry. He had felt the words and fists before about not being an American. That was part of the reason he had gained a reputation as a fighter. He returned people's words with fists and it quieted them. He doubted that they considered or respected him as an American, but they feared and respected him as a fighter—and that was better than nothing.

Coy tried to instill that Mexican-American pride in his children. He realized it was probably an unending battle, but he desperately wanted to win that war of words. He insisted that his Mexican friends and family accept the Butlers because of his acceptance by the Butlers. The Butlers and Coys had bridged the ethnic gap, and Coy wanted others to do the same. Some of Coy's bloodiest fights started because of some stranger's careless racial slurs.

"Dad, do I still have to go to school?" Junior asked.

Coy smiled because he knew there was a diversion somewhere just as with any child.

"Go to school. If you can't talk to the kid or beat him up then let me know," Coy instructed. "That's where most of the prejudice starts anyway, at home."

Jacoba wasn't as educated as Coy's first wife, so she went along with Junior to school in hopes of learning. Coy remembered that one of Bill Butler's children or relatives taught the school. Juan wished he had gone to school so he could read. He recognized just a few words and couldn't write at all. He needed Mrs. Butler around to do his reading and could only scrawl out an "X" for his name. Jacoba couldn't sign her name either, and marked an "X" on official documents.

William G. Butler was not well educated for such a wealthy and powerful man. He taught himself to read and write some but mainly relied on his wife. Butler was strong in common sense and numbers because that was part of business, but he was behind in reading and writing.

Coy didn't think reading was for people like him when he was growing up. He knew it was for priests and teachers, but that was all. A cattle driver and ranch hand didn't need to know such things. He didn't even know how to count past twenty. He just knew when the cattle herd looked a cow or calf short. When he tended just a certain few, it wasn't even a feeling, because he named the cows and knew when one of his family members was missing.

Even that was becoming less and less necessary because of the use of trains. The days of the cattle drive were growing nonexistent, thanks to the railroad. More and more tracks were being laid all across the United States and Texas. The railroad was doing more than just redefining cattle drives. It was bringing the state and nation closer and precipitating a shift in job outlook.

Chapter Twelve

A Tamer West

Juan Coy was loyal to his family and friends, especially the Butlers. But he was also loyal to alcohol and inevitably got into fights with anyone when he was drunk. Because of his size and mere meanness, he very seldom lost. People liked to start drinking with Coy because he was generous with the bottle, but they soon came to recognize the mood change and quickly made their exits when he crossed over that line. Some people were not so lucky.

Coy drank anywhere—San Antonio, Pleasanton, Karnes City, and anywhere in between. Shootouts were still a popular way to settle differences, and Coy killed several people that way. The differences didn't have to be anything major; it could just be an accidental bump in a crowded bar. However, most of the fights started because of gambling.

His family and friends knew the problem and the inevitable results when Coy started drinking. They couldn't always stop him from drinking, but after a while they became more successful at hiding his gun when he was at a bar. He managed to inflict heavy damage with his fists, but at least that wasn't as permanent as a gun.

"Andres, Jacobo, how am I to defend myself in case of a fight?" Juan Coy asked his cousins. "I'll be at a disadvantage if anything happens."

The two San Antonio policemen, who had seen the end results of Juan's fights, just laughed. Fighting an unarmed Juan Coy was as fair as some of the fights got. He had no mercy when he was drunk. More than the worst came out in him.

Both wives dutifully waited for him and cared for him when he had been out on a drinking spree. Being good Mexican wives, they never questioned his motives. He was never violent toward them or their children. Each wife was traditional and obeyed any request of Juan Coy. They knew his reputation and did not want to unleash his wrath.

Mexican women of the era were there to serve their fathers until they married. Then they served their husbands. The women were not allowed to have any opinions in public. They already knew they were to bear many children, raise them, and care for the husband—all without complaining. The husband and wife could walk together when they attended church. But when they were in public, the woman was to walk behind the man, who was obviously the leader.

Coy felt he had the best of all worlds. He was an American with a Mexican culture and background who was born and raised in Texas. He spoke English but not as well as he did Spanish. He even knew some Polish. His main friends were Mexican-American but he was also friendly with many Anglos and Polish people, even some Scandinavians from the nearby community of Cadillac. He encountered his share of discrimination because of his ancestry, but his gun and fists were great equalizers. He killed Anglos, Mexicans, and blacks. In those days blacks were well below Mexicans on the social scale, and killing them was not even considered that much of a crime.

San Antonio in the 1880s had its share of lynchings. A black person who killed an Anglo was almost sure to be dragged from jail by a group of vigilantes during the middle of the night, beaten, and hanged from a tree. The men—usually drunk—then might use him for target practice or slice off a body part as a souvenir. If the black man raped or killed an Anglo woman, he was lucky if he even got to jail. There were mild outcries from the black community but nothing serious. Sometimes, they even supported the lynching and offered to help.

The fifty-year anniversary of the Battle of the Alamo did not bring much attention. There were some small celebrations, in which the Mexican Americans raised more noise than anyone, but Coy did not participate.

Coy had a limited education but urged his children to go further than he had with books. The children carried their load with the family, working on the farm and tending to the house.

Being a Mexican in South Texas, it was natural for Coy to be Catholic. He attended church occasionally and sometimes forgot the "Thou Shalt Not Kill" commandment. The parish priest knew of his reputation and tried converting him to a more peaceful life, after some prodding from both of his wives, but with no luck.

"Father, this is the frontier and people have to protect themselves," Coy remarked. "It's just business."

"I know, my son, but times are changing and the Wild West is growing tamer," the priest said. "Texas is catching up with the civilized world, and it is time you do so also. I remember the days when I myself kept a loaded pistol on the pulpit while I preached."

"I especially remember the time the gun dropped and accidentally went off, Padre," Coy said, and the two men laughed at the distant remembrance.

"That's when I decided the times were getting safer, Juan," the priest said. "When I started making them dangerous was the time to put the trust in God and live life as it is handed to us. We can still protect ourselves, but possessing guns automatically makes us the aggressor."

Coy left the church thinking about their discussion. He attended church occasionally but was still a man who lived by the gun. He had killed at least thirty people and probably would have killed more if it wasn't for his wife, children and, of course, the Butler family. The Butlers did some killing—when it was justified.

Coy was walking around the ranch one evening when Butler wandered up. A train whistle's shrill sound rolled along the hills on the cool, fall evening in 1890.

"Where you off to, Juan?" inquired Butler.

"Nowhere, just getting away from the house," Coy laughed.

Butler nodded and the two walked toward the orange sunset.

"I love noisy houses," Butler reflected. "The more noise there is, the more life there is. Our house was quiet after Emmett got killed. We've both suffered losses. It takes time to get over a friend's death, but I'll never get over Emmett's."

"I hoped the pain would leave after time," Coy said. "It's not something you get over quickly."

"I know, my friend, I'm so sorry about Alejos," Butler said. "It was a shock to us all."

"Yes, yes," Coy muttered in a distant voice. "I still see him at night. I see his face just when he realizes what is happening. I'll see that face forever."

The two had made the fateful journey six years earlier at Christmas. They never talked about it then or even after the burial. This was the first time Juan talked about his own son's death from a hunting accident since that tragic day. The two men who had been through so much together, including the loss of children, were silent for a while.

"It's a shame the railroads are booming so much," Butler changed the subject. "They help so much and make travel so much faster and easier, but it's killing the cowboy and the ranches."

"I thought you did well thanks to the railroads," Coy countered.

"I made some money selling nearby land, and I'm saving money on moving the cattle, but it's not as fun as going for the month-long trail drives. The appeal and challenges are gone. Six states have joined the Union in the last few years, and I've wondered what it would be like out there. I'm sure places like Montana and the Dakotas are still natural and untouched."

"It could be a whole new life, boss," Coy suggested. "That is the life we should be living. Are you thinking of pulling up stakes and moving?"

"I'd love to, but there is no way," Butler declared. "I've built up too much here just to leave, and no one would be willing to pay what it's worth. Besides, moving into a new territory like that would be difficult to just reclaim all of the power I have here. Then, there's convincing the entire family."

"Maybe I should go," offered Coy.

"It wouldn't be good," Butler opined. "They would look at you and think you're an Indian. You'd be shot to death before sundown. They had a whole group of Sioux Indians massacred at Wounded Knee. You're better off here."

"But you're forgetting, Mr. Butler," Coy stopped suddenly and looked directly at Butler. "I'm half Indian. My mother was

A Tamer West 117

William Young (from left), Ildefonso Coy, and Jackson Burris at a hunting ranch circa 1900.
(Photo courtesy of Charlotte Nichols)

William G. Butler sold cattle to Claud Branch and shipped them to Edna, Texas. Note the cattle train in the photo and the town of Karnes City in the background. This photo was taken March 1, 1909, by Conrads Studio.
(The UT Institute of Texan Cultures at San Antonio)

Indian and my father was Mexican. I can't speak the language but I know the life."

"You have family and friends here," Butler said. Butler thought Coy's Indian heritage was what gave his hard edge. He had no stability as a youngster, and it carried over into adulthood.

"I know," Coy muttered, knowing he should keep his family together.

Juan Coy's cousins, Jacobo and Andres, were the best family he had. They looked out for him and tried to get him jobs in law enforcement. When Jacobo and Andres weren't busy with law enforcement, they could drink with the best of them—but not like Juan could.

The three Coys were sitting around a bar in San Antonio one

day. They were at The Star, which was situated on the north side of Commerce Street between the creek and Laredo Street.

"Have you heard about that Jack the Ripper in England?" Jacobo Coy asked no one in particular. "This man has murdered seven women, mainly whores, and taken some of their hearts out. He'd just ripped 'em dead."

"Sickening," Juan replied. "One of 'em must have made him mad. That's just pure torture. Shoot 'em and get it over with. They ever find the guy?"

"Naw, no one ever saw or heard a thing," Andres said. "The women let out a little cry when they were cut, but that's it. Unless he tells someone about it later, he got off."

"I can't see killing a woman anyways unless she done something bad," Juan reasoned. "Seems he wanted to kill just to kill, and he didn't want a fight because otherwise he'd a fought a man. Nope, no sense killing a woman unless she gave him syphilis or cheated on him."

Crimes of passion were still allowed as defense in murder cases, but only if the man killed his wife or her lover. A woman could never retaliate against her husband. It was not uncommon for a man to strike a woman in full public view. People might wince a bit, but they didn't interfere unless it became life threatening.

The Wild West was growing tamer, but the old ways of life would not quickly disappear.

Chapter Thirteen

Visiting San Antonio

Juan Coy enjoyed his trips to San Antonio. The Grand Opera House, and all the other saloons in town, provided entertainment and whiskey. They also kept him occupied with fist fights when the whiskey warmed him up enough.

But Coy also enjoyed San Antonio for the excitement of being in Texas' largest city (25,000 people). A country boy in attitude and thinking, Coy was amazed at San Antonio's size, opportunities, and diversity. There were some people and areas that weren't tolerant of Mexicans or African Americans, but there were other areas where the diversity flourished. San Antonio had areas where Coy thought he was in another country. The town's population consisted mainly of Anglos, Germans, and Mexicans. There were also small, separate areas of Italians, blacks, Irish, Polish, and Chinese. In some places English and Spanish were rarely spoken. The architecture showed signs of Europe, and the ethnic food was always a treat. Each culture had its own alcoholic beverages, and Coy enjoyed the different kinds of beer. His overall cultural favorites were the Polish area and the area called Irish Flats. He was accepted in both areas.

Coy didn't care for the Germans who established themselves in San Antonio in the 1850s. They were strict disciplinarians and hard-working individuals who were very cliquish. Not only did they keep to themselves, but they even ostracized other Germans who didn't measure up to their working standards. That was probably one reason Coy enjoyed the Polish community. They were escaping German oppression in Europe. He didn't care for the Chinese, who moved into the area in 1890. They didn't drink, and they also kept to themselves.

Coy could get lost in San Antonio. His reputation was known throughout Karnes and Wilson counties and all around the area covering Floresville, Kenedy, Helena, and Pleasanton. Every worker at every saloon in that South Texas area knew Coy by sight and knew that trouble usually followed. He was restricted on his drinking, not just because of the saloon's own common sense but under William Butler's orders. Butler didn't want his friend and hired gun getting in any more trouble than he already had. At least in San Antonio, he could blend in with all the other people.

There were more saloons in San Antonio than houses in Floresville. If Coy wore out his welcome at one place, he could easily stagger across the street into another saloon. Another good thing about San Antonio was that if he was kicked out of one saloon, he could stay away for a week and then return. Most saloons had so many people coming in and out that it was difficult for the bartenders to remember one particular person.

Coy remembered well a trip he took to San Antonio with his wife and newborn child on July 7, 1891. Jacoba brought along little Alejos, who was just ten weeks old. Coy dropped off his horse and carriage at a downtown livery station so they could enjoy the streetcar ride from downtown to San Pedro Park. They brought a change of clothes so they could swim in the springs. Juan and Jacoba enjoyed the day at the park as they waded around the pool with Alejos, walked around the zoo, and ate a picnic dinner. The family even visited the Museum of Natural History.

Juan wanted to take a balloon ride but decided against it. The streetcar ride cost him 15 cents and the museum 25 cents. The family enjoyed the picnic dinner on the park grounds and, finally with the sun going down at 7:15 P.M., they rolled out their blankets and prepared for the overnight camping adventure. Attendants came by at 7:30 P.M. on the dot to light the gaslights. The whole process startled the children in the park, who had never seen such a sight. They were used to the gas lamps at home and knew the process by heart.

They saw the wick but couldn't see the lamp oil which kept it lit. Coy explained to a couple of children who had rolled out blankets close to his that there was a nearby tank holding the oil and that underground pipes brought the gas to the lamp.

A dozen families camped out at San Pedro Park that night. It was enjoyable camping out under the stars so close to the city and action. There were campfires all around the park with some people singing, others telling stories, and others just sitting back enjoying the sights. Some wandered around the grounds, visiting friends and enjoying the stars.

"Children, did you know this park is the oldest one this side of the Mississippi River?" Coy asked the two children as they gathered around the fire. "This park is more than 150 years old. It was a park long before the United States even declared its independence from England. The U.S. military used the park during the Mexican-American War, and the Confederates used it for a prison camp during the Civil War."

"Mister, did you fight in those wars?" asked one child.

"I did fight some in the Civil War," Coy reflected. "I was too young for most of it. But I did get to march a lot."

"I don't like wars," the other child said. "You can get hurt."

Coy looked at the child and smiled.

"Did you ride your horse here?" asked the first child.

"We rode a streetcar out here today. The streetcar and the donkey belong to the city and we'll ride both of them back to town tomorrow."

"Do you know any ghost stories, mister?"

"Just a short one but not too scary," Coy laughed. "This is a true story. You remember the Alamo. It started out as a church back in the 1700s and was still a church when they had the famous fight there. The Mexicans killed the men at the Alamo back before I was born, but your grandpa probably remembers when it happened. After it was all over, a Mexican general wanted to burn the Alamo down so no one could go back into the church. The general gave the orders to his men to burn it so the men grabbed torches and approached the building. But as soon as they got close to the building, Colonel Travis, Davy Crockett, and Jim Bowie came out from the walls and told them not to burn the Alamo. The soldiers were so scared, they dropped their torches and ran away. That's why the Alamo is still standing."[1]

"Are you sure?" asked one of the wide-eyed youngsters.

"Of course, *mijo*. The Alamo has been a lot of things during the years. The Alamo was here long ago just like this park. It started out as a church, then after the battle it was used as a storage center for the army. God doesn't like churches to be torn down."

The next morning after a hearty breakfast, the Coy family rode the streetcar back downtown. Juan had a meeting with his attorney and a doctor in a bid to receive a Civil War pension.

Coy met with his attorney, E. B. Johnson, in the Howard Building on Soledad Street, which was down from the courthouse. The two had discussed the pension at a meeting the previous November. Johnson advised Coy that he needed witnesses to his service in L Company's First Texas Union Cavalry and a doctor's examination report. Ordinarily, the doctor's exam would be in Austin, but Johnson received a waiver for Coy to be examined in San Antonio since he had already traveled sixty-three miles from his home at Kenedy Junction.

Dr. Joseph Jones noted Coy's vitals signs: pulse, 78; respiration, 18; temperature, 98.5; height: 5-feet-4½; weight, 175; age, 49.[2] Coy had been suffering from inflammatory rheumatism the last four years and had been wearing a cut boot or shoe on his left foot due to the constant swelling.[3]

Jones wrote that he could find no disability due to the knife wound and could not make a required rating.[4] Coy retained Johnson as his lawyer on September 6, 1890, for a $10 fee in handling the Declaration for Invalid Pension. Johnson wrote that Coy was "one-half" unable to support himself through manual labor because of the rheumatism and knife wound.[5]

After Coy was examined and made his mark on the necessary paperwork that Wednesday, he and Jacoba carried little Alejos around town. They enjoyed sightseeing and touring the shopping area. They finally stopped in at one store.

"Oh, Juan, please let's get some ice cream," urged Jacoba. "I want one of those Dolly Vardens."

"A Dolly what?"

"A Dolly Varden. It's ice cream with some soda," Jacoba said. "It's real good."

"Okay, sounds good to me."

The three of them sat at a booth and ordered two Dolly Vardens. The woman returned with two frosty glasses with brown foam at the top and a white glob of ice cream in the middle. Jacoba held Alejos and fed him small spoonfuls of ice cream.

"Oooh, my head hurts," Juan declared. "It's like my brain has frozen. Maybe I shouldn't eat it so fast."

"I'm sorry, I forgot to tell you about that," Jacoba apologized. "This is the first time you've had ice cream, isn't it?"

Juan looked a little ashamed before nodding a yes. "First time for soda, too."

The two finished their Dolly Vardens and looked around the shop for a few minutes before leaving. They made their plans outside the store as Jacoba and Alejos headed off to look for clothes while Juan went to a barber shop.

The barber shop on South Flores was already filled with customers. Both barbers were busy clipping hair and shaving beards, and there were still four other men sitting and chatting who were ahead of Coy. The men stopped talking and looked at Coy a few seconds as he entered the small shop with the glass front.

"Shave and a cut please," Coy asked politely as he entered the shop. One barber nodded and Coy sat down in a chair. Soon the entire group was chatting away again. Most of the discussion was about local politics and happenings that did not interest Coy. It was rather relaxing for him since he was away from his reputation as Butler's hired gun. Some people knew him in the Sporting District, but this was the shopping and business section of town. He was just another citizen here, and that suited him just fine.

Chapter Fourteen

"Shoot me if you can..."

Capt. Lee Hall called upon his old friend, William Butler, to help with a strike that was crippling his railroad. The railroad was trying to run with the help of some sympathetic workers, management, and some recent employees, but there was strong resistance from strikers. Hall asked Butler for the services of Juan Coy.

"Juan Coy is the kind of man I need riding the rails and guarding the depots," Hall pleaded with Butler. "I'll pay him more than what you're paying him right now. Colonel, I need the man."

"So I've heard," Butler remarked as he poured a shot of bourbon into Hall's empty glass. "The strike has hurt a lot and it doesn't seem like you've been getting many breaks. Do you think it will be over soon?"

"It should be over in the next couple of months, but it's what happens in the meantime that has me worried," Hall said as he lifted the glass to his lips. He knocked back a hefty sip, breathed a sigh, then placed the glass on the table. "Good Kentucky whiskey, Bill. Coy will settle things down just by his presence and word will spread."

"I believe you, Captain, and I'll ask him . . ." Butler hesitated. "But don't be surprised if he says no. Juan remarried a couple of years ago and they have a little boy, less than a year old. He's almost a changed man. He limps some and rheumatism slows him a bit. He stays at home more."

"Can I at least ask him?" Hall countered. "Will you tell him first that it's okay? He has total respect for you."

"Lee, you know me. I'll help you any way possible," Butler said. "I'm just saying it's not as easy as it was to get Coy."

Butler sent one of his servants out in the field to find Coy. The servant found Coy shodding a horse in the barn. The servant filled Coy in on some of the information that he had overheard between Hall and Butler. Coy was noncommittal and just nodded.

Hall extended his hand as Coy entered the room. Butler offered Coy some coffee. All three men sat in the overstuffed chairs in Butler's living room as Hall began his speech while Coy sipped some coffee. Hall was just a few minutes into his speech about the atrocities happening with the railroad, the injuries, the chance of more danger, and the possibility of a quick end if Coy helped, when Coy interrupted him.

"If you're looking for help in guarding the railroad, I'll do it," Coy smiled. "I'll do it for two weeks at a time, then I want to come home for a few days. I have a little boy and I don't want to miss his growing up too much."

The three men stood and shook hands. They sat back down and ironed out some details on what Coy was to do, where he was to report, and how much money he would make.

Hall returned to San Antonio. He instructed Coy and the others as to where they would go for the first day of work and what each would be doing. Hall told Coy he would be working with his cousin, Jesse Perez again. Perez was a member of the Texas Rangers Company B under Capt. Lee Hall at the time of the strike.[1] Perez had just finished working a case with Pablino Coy, who was shot in the hip. Pablino Coy fired back and killed Manual Ochoa instantly.[2] Perez was ordered to the Southern Hotel, in San Antonio, where he met up with Captain Hall. Only six Rangers were able to leave San Antonio for Houston in order to protect the railroad.[3]

Hall could enlist as many as he needed so he signed up three people in Floresville and proceeded to Kenedy, where he picked up more deputies, including Sykes and William Butler, along with Ildefonso, Emmett, and Juan Coy. Hall closed every door on the train and had Rangers on each car platform to ward off the 1,200 strikers who were present. There were shouts and threats but no violence. Half of the Rangers were dropped off at Yoakum.[4]

The sabotage was anything from greasing the tracks to placing logs on them in the hopes of derailment. Also, soda was added to the engine, which caused it to explode. Perez was up in front with the engineer when it exploded. The engineer said the engine was on the verge of exploding even more. Perez decided to bail out. He took his Winchester and, remembering there was a lake on both sides of the tracks, jumped from the train. The train couldn't go any farther so they had to wait there for another train. Some Rangers operated a handcart to Houston in order to bring back another engine. The next day, when Perez was walking around the lake, he was shocked to discover a fourteen-foot alligator in the lake.[5]

It wasn't until the second day that another engine arrived and they resumed their trip to Houston. Perez got off the train in Yoakum, in order to guard the station and a water tank outside the city.[6] After a stay in Yoakum, Perez was sent to Waco. A man carrying a Colt .45 hopped on the train and pointed the gun at the engineer. Perez had the jump on him and leveled his gun at the man, disarming him.[7]

"Who are you?" questioned Perez.

"I'm the sheriff and you're in trouble," replied the man.

"We'll find out who you are in a few minutes when the train stops," Perez said. "We'll just go to the sheriff's office to find out who you are."

The train stopped and the two men departed for the sheriff's office. Once there, some deputies recognized the sheriff and forced him loose from Perez' grasp.[8]

"Now, you are under arrest," the sheriff said, each word growing louder. "You can take that cell over there."

Capt. Lee Hall showed up with sixteen soldiers, explained the situation, and requested Perez' release. The soldiers accompanied Perez to the train station and he was headed for Yoakum.[9]

A week later, Perez was ordered to Waco again. Juan Coy requested and was granted permission to join Perez on the trip to Waco. They arrived about 3:00 A.M. Coy told Perez to stay in the caboose while he stayed with the engineer up front. Coy walked around outside to stretch his legs, and it wasn't long before the sheriff appeared and pointed a gun at Coy's head.[10]

"Gotcha right where I want you," boasted the sheriff.

"You got the wrong man," Coy said. "I don't know you."

The sheriff lowered his gun a bit and took a closer look at Coy in the full moon.

"Sorry, I do have the wrong man," the sheriff apologized. "Please forgive me."

That was all the break Coy needed. Coy had his gun out in a flash and aimed right between the sheriff's eyes. The sheriff was shocked. Coy reached and took the sheriff's gun.[11] Coy motioned for the sheriff to walk ahead.

"Stop here." Coy stopped in front of a boxcar. "Step up here. Get comfortable." He pulled the door shut and locked the boxcar. Coy then ran down to the caboose to get Perez.

"What the hell you been doing?" Perez questioned.

"I got a prisoner and he's got the nicest looking gun," Coy said as he displayed the gun to his cousin. "Take a look at him and see if he's some tramp. If he's some bum, we'll turn him loose."

Perez studied the gun carefully and it looked rather familiar. But then he was a lawman and each make looked similar after a while. Coy went to the boxcar and opened it. The sheriff was fuming.

"You, again," the sheriff yelled at Perez. "You're in deep trouble."

"That's pretty strong for someone who doesn't have a gun," Coy said. "Get down and start walking."

Perez poked the sheriff's gun in his own back and the two men started walking. Captain Hall was not too far away.

"Who in the hell are you, anyway?" Hall yelled. "You have interfered with my men long enough. It's a wonder they haven't killed you yet. Juan, you must be getting soft. Sheriff, I'm sending you to San Antonio, where your life will be miserable."

The captain kept his word, placing the poor Waco sheriff on the next train to San Antonio without money or a gun. It took a while for the sheriff to get back to Waco, but Perez and Coy were long gone by then.[12]

A group of Hall's men, including Coy, went to San Antonio, pulling into town about 11:00 P.M. The first thing they did was to visit the Bella Union Theater on Dolorosa and Laredo streets. At 3:00 that morning, Perez and Coy left the Bella Union and crossed the street to a restaurant that was run by Mrs. Juanita Garza. Coy ordered a breakfast of bacon, eggs, toast, and coffee. Perez ordered eggs, beans, toast, and milk. Henry Krempkau, who had just left his brother Albert's saloon, entered the restaurant shortly after Coy, sat down at a table, and motioned Garza to come over.[13]

"I'll be with you in a minute," Garza offered. "I'm fixing Mr. Coy's breakfast."[14]

"Who in the hell is Mr. Coy?" yelled Krempkau.[15] "Bring me coffee now."

Coy didn't say a word. He could tell the man had been drinking. Coy could have ended the discussion right then with one punch, but he didn't feel like fighting. Besides, Coy didn't have his gun and he always liked to have backup to his fists. Coy looked at Perez and the other men. He quietly got up from the table, fished out a couple of coins, placed them on the table, and walked away.[16]

Coy was on loan from Butler to his old friend, Capt. Lee Hall, to protect the San Antonio and Aransas Pass Railroad's property while its workers were on strike.[17] Coy was stationed in Yoakum and had worked there twenty-five days when he decided he wanted some of his money so he could go home. He settled with the railroad superintendent but was unable to get his money that Monday morning. He was planning to spend a few days with his family before returning to work in Yoakum.[18]

Coy, forty-nine years old and growing weary of the gunman's lifestyle he had gained through the years, now enjoyed spending time with his family, particularly his youngest child. Alejos was not even a year old, but Juan enjoyed just holding him and rocking him to sleep. Victoriano and Juan Junior stayed near home and tried to build something of a ranch with their father. Juan was looking to the future when he could spend time at home on his ranch, with his wife, and have the children and, eventually grandchildren, visit him on the land loaned from Mr. Butler.

Perez met up with Coy about 4:00 that Monday afternoon. He was going home and invited Coy along for the ride. Coy refused.[19]

"I'll just stay around here," Coy said. "I want my money so I can go home for a few days. Tell my favorite aunt I said hello. We're gonna go have some drinks later."

"I've got to go home," Perez said. "My folks know I'm in town and I'll have hell to pay if I don't stop in. Leal is coming with me because he lives close by."

Coy's trip home would have to be put off another day, so he decided to spend it like he had many others—in a bar. He wound up at Albert Krempkau's saloon on Dolorosa and South Laredo streets. He had been there just a short time when two scabs, or strike-breakers, joined him in the saloon. The two scabs were refused service.[20] Word got around fast when it came to such issues. Unions were still in their infancy, but the attitude and support were already strong.

"Two whiskeys, barkeep," ordered one of the scabs.

Krempkau kept silent in the corner, staring straight ahead. He had served Coy because he knew of his reputation and had seen it in action before. But the scabs would have to find some other place. Krempkau knew it would be dangerous for business if it became a scabs' hangout or even sympathetic to the scabs. His clientele were rowdy and drunk, which included law enforcement officers. Coy was still a deputy sheriff in Wilson County and liked to flash the badge to gain some respect and privileges. The rowdy bunch of drinkers could stand killings and fights but couldn't tolerate scabs. Krempkau would be out of business if word got out about him siding with the scabs.

"Hey, are you going to serve my friends?" Coy yelled as he slammed his glass on the bar. "They want some whiskey. Now give it to them."

"Who are you to come in here and tell me what to do?" Krempkau retorted. He had been sampling the inventory quite a bit himself. He suffered from rheumatism[21] and the alcohol killed the pain. "For a short Mexican, you sure talk a lot. I know who you are, but you don't scare me. You didn't scare my brother, either."

"That's all you can think of—a short Mexican? For one of those hard-working, supposedly intelligent Germans that's all you can come up with," Coy laughed. "I don't care what you think. Just give them the drink. You've been taking my money, now I'm giving you more to give them whiskey."

"Juan, let's go, he's not worth the trouble," one man pleaded. "It's because of the railroad strike."

"He's right, John. We'll go some other place," the other agreed. They tried to get up, but Coy pulled them back down.

Coy had been drinking at the saloon for several years and had had run-ins with Krempkau before. Thinking back, Coy probably shot up the place or got into at least a fight or two, but then who hadn't gotten rowdy in a saloon?

The Mexican taunts Coy heard were typical when he was in certain parts of San Antonio. It wasn't a problem when he was back in Floresville and Karnes County. His old friend Bill Butler respected him and his heritage. Coy had grown to tolerate the taunts when he was in San Antonio. But this was coming from Krempkau, who was despised by some Germans.

The Germans had been in Texas approximately forty years and had made an impact with their clothing manufacturing and selling, carpentry, construction, farming, and attention to fine detail. They had taken over many jobs because of their tireless work ethics and fine detailed organizational skills. Few Germans settled in San Antonio, though, as they chose to stay close together north of San Antonio in such communities as New Braunfels and Spechts. There was a small group of Germans in the King William area. No Germans lived south of town because that was mainly the Polish community. Those two groups did not mix well at all.

"No, we're staying," Coy declared. "If my money is good enough for my drinks then it's good enough for the two of you."

"Listen to your friends, Juan," Krempkau chided. "Since when did you become John? A Mexican trying to become an American. Hell, I've seen everything now."

"I'm just as American as you, born and raised here in Texas and the United States," Coy reasoned. "My parents were here in Texas before your family even heard of the country."

"You may have lived here longer, but I belong. You have nothing and you never will. I work and buy things. You just take things. I'm a contributing member of society. You, you're just a menace to the society."

"I've had enough, Krempkau. Let's go outside," Coy urged.

"No, we'll stay inside," Krempkau replied. The cocky look was soon fading.

"Are you scared? You know I'll beat the breath right out of that sorry body of yours," Coy said. "Let's go outside because I don't want to damage your bar that much, just you."

The two scabs tried to grab hold of Coy's arms and lead him away from trouble. But it was too late. The other bar patrons circled around Coy with whiskey and beer glasses in hand, looking for excitement. Less than a dozen people gathered near the bar, shouting encouragement for a fight. Most of the people in the bar were strikers and in full support of Krempkau. Jacobo Coy, Juan's cousin, was in the crowd, too, and heard some of the excitement.

"Juan, let it go," Jacobo urged. "Albert isn't worth it. Go some other place."

Coy shook his head at his cousin as he pushed his bar stool away and headed toward the door. Coy stepped gingerly with his swollen left foot.

"Outside . . . let's go out and fight in the street like real men," yelled Coy. He walked with his back toward the door and opened up the duster he was wearing to show he was not armed. "C'mon, I'm not armed," urged Coy.

Krempkau walked from out behind the counter, grabbing his pistol out of his holster, on the way. Krempkau leveled the pistol at Coy, who was standing in the doorway holding the door open.

"C'mon . . . shoot. I'm not armed, but I'm not scared like you are, either. Shoot me if you can."

Krempkau kept advancing and was twelve feet away from Coy. The crowd followed Krempkau at a safe distance. They had seen Coy before and did not know if he was telling the truth about being armed or not. Even if he didn't have a gun, he could have a long hunting knife. Krempkau's pistol was shaking slightly in his hand as he squeezed the trigger.

The wood on the doorway splintered just a split second after the pop from the gun sounded. The wood sound was followed immediately by Coy's laughter.

"Come on, shoot again. I'll give you another chance. You can't do it. Shoot me again."

Coy and Krempkau were now outside on Laredo Street. Patrons from other bars headed cautiously outside in search of the gunfire. San Antonio Police Officer Ed Sarran ran across the street when he heard the shot. Coy kept his coat open and arms outstretched as a target.[22] He turned around as if a spindletop. Krempkau continued toward Coy, raised the gun once again, and fired. Coy was still in midturn when the ball struck him in the left hip and exited from his back.[23]

The shot stunned him and even staggered him somewhat. The ball did not strike any major artery or any bone. Coy slumped into

Sarran's arms but remained standing.[24] Krempkau backed into his bar somewhat, but kept his eyes on Coy. Krempkau could still see Coy over the swinging door.

"That's all?" Coy laughed. "Shoot again. Go ahead, shoot again! You don't have the guts."

"Drop the gun, Albert," Sarran ordered. "You've done enough. Now drop the gun."

"I can't, I'm afraid he'll kill me," Krempkau said.

"He won't kill you, I won't let him," Sarran said. "Drop it. You've already wounded him."

"He won't kill me now. He'll wait till later. I have to finish him now or be killed later."

Krempkau leveled the gun and fired at Coy, who was still standing thanks to the aid of Officer Ed Sarran. Coy was still displaying himself as a target. Despite the limp from the shot to the hip, Coy still circled his arms around, although not as pronounced as earlier. He was acting like a bird in flight. Krempkau's third shot went into Coy's right shoulder, severed a main artery near the clavicle, penetrated another artery closer to the heart, and went out under his left arm.[25]

Coy was dead instantly.

Sarran, who was holding onto Coy, was hit in the left hand when the ball exited Coy. It was a slight flesh wound.[26]

Sarran carefully slid Coy down to the sidewalk and allowed the blood to spurt out of the open shoulder wound. It was more of a gusher with the artery severed the way it was. There was no life remaining in Juan Coy.

San Antonio Police Officer Jacob Ripps walked into the saloon and up to the counter where Krempkau was standing and immediately arrested him.[27] Krempkau surrendered his pistol.

Sarran went to get a doctor, but he knew it wasn't necessary. He was also going to notify the city police office and the coroner's office. Ripps searched Coy's body and discovered a small, closed pocketknife.

"That's all he had, Albert," Ripps held up the knife. "A simple, little pocketknife that any kid carries."[28]

"You don't understand," Krempkau pleaded as Ripps led him away for the short trip to the jail. "He can kill at any time. Look at all of the other men he has killed."

Perez was blocks away at his parents' house but heard the distinct gun shots. He rode his horse downtown and met up with Antonio Sandoval, who told him how Albert Krempkau shot and killed Coy. Perez continued over to Laredo and Dolorosa streets, joining the crowd that waited for the justice of the peace, Anton Adams, to pick up Coy.[29]

A crowd from the saloons, show palaces and nearby sporting houses immediately gathered at the corner of Laredo and Dolorosa streets to view the body. They heard the shooting and honed in on the sound. People of all nationalities and ages gathered around the body, whispering about who it was and how the shooting occurred.[30] Once they realized it was Juan Coy, the whispering got louder from the stories about the man.

"Good . . . it's about time someone stood up to him," said one man.

"I hope they make a hero out of who did this," another said. "They should never arrest anyone for cleaning up the town."

"Coy was a pure troublemaker," added another man. "He came up here to stir up trouble and then went back south for his peace and quiet."

"I heard he killed more than fifty men," one woman offered.

"I heard it was more than a hundred and that he had helped in killing President Garfield," one gentleman exaggerated.

Meanwhile, Ripps was busy interviewing some of the witnesses to the murder. One of the bar patrons present was Jacobo Coy, Juan's cousin. The two Coys weren't drinking together but they had exchanged pleasantries whenever they passed each other in the bar. Jacobo was still an officer, with the San Antonio Police Department, and served as special agent.

"I heard the argument, but that's just the way Juan always was," Jacobo told the officer. "I told him he should leave. I didn't think it would progress to a shooting. He had been drinking a while and arguing for half that time. I don't know why he would just challenge Krempkau to shoot him like that. I thought he was going to get into a fist fight with him.

"This wouldn't have happened if it hadn't been for what I did yesterday," Jacobo continued. "We were at the Bella Union theater yesterday, and after he had been drinking for half an hour I told him it was dangerous and irresponsible for him to still be carrying his gun. He admitted that the bottle could get the best of him, and he didn't always realize he was that dangerous when he was drinking. So he gave the bartender the gun for safekeeping,[31] but he never retrieved it because he went to breakfast early this morning and slept most of the day. The bartender gave me the gun, but I never gave it back to him. He has become more responsible lately with the gun and drinking. He doesn't mix the two like he did."

Justice of the Peace Adams pushed his way through the crowd to examine the body and the crime scene. He tried to get the people to back away but was constantly smothered by the group. It was extremely difficult for him to begin his coroner's inquest.[32] Adams ordered the body taken to Sheero's establishment, where the crowd continued to gather and gawk at the fallen man.[33] It wasn't until an hour later that the black hearse came by to pick up Coy. Again, the officers had to fight through the crowd that formed a human barricade on the sidewalk. It was past 9:00 P.M. but the crowd continued to gather in large numbers. Adams ordered the undertaker to take Coy to the morgue and prepare him for burial.[34]

The undertaker undressed Coy and examined the body. One gun wound was on the left side. The bullet had struck the spine and exited in the middle of the back. This was the first gunshot wound Coy received from Krempkau and the one that forced him to prop himself against the wall and Officer Sarran. The second shot—the fatal shot—struck the middle of the left shoulder, just missing the jugular vein. That shot went downward, hit bone, and came out in the back of the right shoulder. The undertaker determined that the weapon used was a .44-caliber pistol.[35]

Juan Coy went back to Floresville on the train that Tuesday afternoon of January 26, 1892, but without the pay he had gone to San Antonio seeking.

At the time of his death, Coy was under indictment for killing a black man in Floresville seven years before.[36] Despite being under indictment, Coy had continued to work with the city police, marshal and sheriff offices. The fact that it was a black man didn't rush the case to court. The charges stemming from the Daileyville Riot had been dropped after the hung jury. Coy had served five years in prison for killing Luciano Cantu.

Perez said of his cousin years later: ". . . John Coy, was a fearless man, he was not [scared] of nothing. That was the reason he was killed . . ."³⁷ A normal person who was unarmed wouldn't have challenged someone with a pistol. If so, they surely would have run after the first missed shot.

No one was really shocked that Coy had been killed, and many expressed a sigh of relief that he was finally gone. Jacobo and Ildefonso Coy, who had both tried to steer Juan in new directions but with little luck, accompanied Juan's body back to Floresville. They went to his house to notify his wife, but word had already reached her. She was crying in the front room when Jacobo and Ildefonso came calling with the bad news. She held the baby, who was also crying. Mr. and Mrs. Butler were there to lend support. Jacobo and Ildefonso brought the casket with them from San Antonio and carried it into the house. Burial would be the next day, at the Lodi Cemetery, in back of the Catholic church property.³⁸

The funeral service and burial, in Lodi, were well attended by the Coys and Butlers, with cousins from San Antonio joining those from Floresville and Karnes City. The *San Antonio Daily Express* reported that Coy was buried Wednesday, January 27, and that he had a wife and one child but no other relatives.³⁹ Juan wasn't an active member of any church but his wife, who was a God-fearing woman and attended mass regularly, talked a priest into leading a service. The wind whipped through the trees from the southeast and brought more of a chill to everyone in the fifty-five-degree weather.

William Butler led the group in a singing of "Amazing Grace," which many saw fitting.

"Juan Coy was a friend of mine," Butler eulogized. "A man I was proud to know and trust through many years. He was a hard-living man, a man with many faults, but whatever bad things you may say about him must be countered with good things such as how he was a loving, family man and one who had many friends. His word was his bond. He tried to help those needy people for that is how he died, fighting for respect of two people less fortunate than him. Those two men will remember Juan Coy forever and how he stood up for them that night. We will also remember him for the lifetime of support he gave us. His wife and sons will remember him as a loving and caring husband and father."

Coy had been waiting for his pay from the San Antonio and Aransas Pass paymaster. That was why he was still in San Antonio, despite having settled with the superintendent earlier that Monday. The *San Antonio Daily Express* reported on January 31 that the paymaster who was supposed to have paid off that Monday, January 25, was finally "paying off the boys as rapidly as possible" on January 30. "There are a large number of old men who are due their pay for December and who are anxiously awaiting the time when Paymaster Wagner will pay them," it was reported.[40]

Jacoba Reyes was fifteen years old when she married Juan Coy and just sixteen years old when she had their first and only child, Alejos. She became a widow at the age of seventeen. Nine years later, she married Juan de los Reyes on May 30, 1901.[41] The three older Coy boys were already out living on their own when Alejos was born in 1891. Alejos, who wasn't even a year old when his father was killed, lived with the Perez family and others after his father died. The 1900 census has Alejos living with his uncle, Tomas Travieso, in Wilson County. Even after his mother remarried, Alejos did not spend that much time with his mother and stepfather. She died in 1954 at the age of seventy-nine and is buried in San Antonio.

Jacoba filed more paperwork on Juan Coy's pension claim, which he had started a year before his death. The government rejected the widow's claim because the marriage certificate notes the wedding was July 23, 1890, almost a month after the act's passage on June 27, 1890.[42]

Juan Coy had four sons from his first marriage and one son from his second marriage. His first wife, Manuela Rios, whom he married in Floresville in 1867, bore him Victoriano, Antonio, Juan, and Alejos. The Alejos born to Manuela died in a hunting accident when he was fourteen years old. The lone child born to Jacoba Reyes, his second wife, was named after the Alejos who died in a hunting accident.

Victoriano, Juan's oldest son, was born in 1869 and died in 1954 at age eighty-five. He and his wife, Juanita, had thirteen children—Juan, Manuel, Blas, José, Antonio, Isabel, Ines, Aurelia, Jesus, Paulina, David, Andres, and Victor, Jr. Andres was born in 1919, and then there was a ten-year gap before Victor, Jr., the last child, was born. The family lived in Atascosa County until 1912 and then moved to Bastrop County.

Juan Coy II had two sons, Juan III and Alejos, who played baseball. There is no other information on his side of the family.

Apparently Antonio Coy inherited some of his father's traits as far as a temper and a killer. Juan, Antonio, and another man were sitting around when a passerby insulted Antonio. "*Vez ese? Es hijo de un perro bravo.*"[43] (You see him? He is the son of a mad dog.) Antonio took exception to the remark, grabbed a large knife, and stabbed the man to death. He fled San Antonio, only to return for an occasional visit. No information is known on how long he lived, where he moved to, or if he ever married and had children.

Alejos Coy died in 1967 at the age of seventy-five. His first child was named Johnny. His other children were named Alex, Rudolfo, Victoria, Estella, Odel, and Olivia.

CHAPTER FIFTEEN

End of a Violent Era

The death of Juan Coy was page-one news in San Antonio as reported in *The Daily Light* of Tuesday, January 26, 1892, but the story was inside the *San Antonio Daily Express*. It also garnered four paragraphs in that day's *New York Times*. The *Times*' story was rather brutal in its portrayal of Coy, calling him a "Mexican desperado."[1] The stories not only detailed the killing of Coy but also his life and how he had put an end to so many lives himself. The *Times* ran the name of Henry, Albert's brother, as the assailant. The headline read "Juan Coy Shot" and "A Saloon Keeper Ends the Life of a Border Ruffian."[2]

The story related how Henry Krempkau killed Coy, "one of the most notorious fighters the frontier of Texas has produced." The single shot fired from a Colt six-shooter broke the desperado's neck. "He never spoke afterward," the *Times* reported.[3] "Coy entered the saloon in a semi-intoxicated condition and got in a dispute with the proprietor over some trivial matter. The argument grew warm, and Coy reached for his knife, intending to disembowel his adversary. Krempkau was too quick."[4]

The story described Coy as being of "Mexican lineage, some forty years old, and married." The contrasts of him sober and drunk were fairly accurate. "The exact record of his killings is not obtainable. They are known to have been pretty numerous." The article mentioned the shootout in Daileyville and how "a little while after, he killed a man named Trevino in Wilson County. He was under indictment for murder in De Witt County."[5]

It's a wonder that anyone from New York would even venture into Texas after reading the final paragraph: "Coy was a typical representative of the Mexican desperado, who differs from the American in the same line of business in that he is always more savage and fearless. He was known throughout a territory as large as the State of New York, and wherever known, was feared."[6]

Such a story was typical fodder for the New York press about the ways of the Wild West. Many of the items in the story were true, but some were fictional. There were no accounts of Coy reaching for his knife, much less any plans to disembowel anyone. The knife was not discovered until after he was dead. The knife was just a simple pocketknife[7] that any man of that time—and since then—would carry in his pocket for general purposes. That kind of knife would barely disembowel a small animal and especially not a living, moving human being. The story provided the only mention about Coy being under indictment for murder in DeWitt County.

Surprisingly, there was even an editorial written about the shooting, stating that Coy's life should have been spared and that the police were partly to blame for his death. The editorial in the January 28, 1892, issue of the *San Antonio Daily Express* stated that apparently one officer reported hearing the argument break out between Coy and Krempkau but did nothing to stop it. The editorial suggested that, if the story was true, the officer should at least be stripped of his badge and possibly held as an accessory:[8] ". . . for if he had performed his sworn duty by arresting the aggressive party promptly when the first insulting or threatening word was given, the tragedy could have been prevented. The trouble with too many police officers is that they do not seem to consider it their duty to interfere and they can take a smoking pistol or blood-dripping knife from the hands of one, and the other fellow has keeled over with a hole through him or his bowels protruding from a knife wound. Insulting or abusive language is as much an infraction of the law, and the prompt arrest of such offenders would stop quarrels and prevent fighting; but the officer too often stands idle until the aggrieved party, finding his other protection from his assailant, meets it with a blow or a shot, when he finds that he has, in addition to be insulted by an enemy, also been arrested by the officer who failed to do his duty in the first instance."[9]

It was reported in the *San Antonio Daily Express* of January 31, 1892, that the Bexar County grand jury indicted Krempkau for first-degree murder, in the Juan Coy killing.[10]

On February 1, the *Express* reported the 37th District Court's criminal docket for early February included the State against Jacobo Coy, Miguel Coy, and Antonio Coy on charges of gambling. Antonio Coy pleaded guilty and was sentenced to ten days in jail and a $25 fine.[11] The status of the cases against Jacobo and Miguel Coy was never found.

The February 13, 1892, *San Antonio Daily Express* reported that Albert Krempkau's habeas corpus proceeding was to begin that day. Krempkau was still imprisoned in the Bexar County Jail. Krempkau talked to a reporter the prior evening. "The time has been long to him and he was anxiously looking for the dawn of to-day when he will have a hearing. He gave no statement of the shooting but felt confident that he would come out all right in to-day's hearing. The evidence given before Justice [Anton] Adam for the state he did not consider very damaging, except in the instance of one other witness. He hardly expected that the case would be finished during the day."[12]

Krempkau's habeas corpus case reached court on February 13, with John A. Green and Robert Green representing him.[13]

Charles Richter testified that he heard words between Coy and Krempkau, which included a quarrel Coy had earlier that day with Henry Krempkau, Albert's brother. Richter said he then heard Coy challenge Albert Krempkau to a fight and proceeded out into the street.[14]

"'Come outside and I can whip you,'" Richter reported Coy telling Krempkau. After that, Coy headed back into the saloon, according to Richter, but a shot was fired.[15]

"'Shoot again, you ——, I am not dead yet,'" Richter continued with Coy's reply.[16]

"Coy was advancing toward the saloon and continued to do so even after the second shot was fired," the newspaper reported of Richter's testimony. "When Coy first entered the saloon, a witness had seen a knife in his hand, partly concealed up his sleeve. He had also demanded a cigarette which one of the men in the saloon, named Henry Kusler, was smoking, and the latter gave it up."[17]

Richter was quoted as saying he did not know Coy's condition at the time "but he looked as if he was looking for a row."[18]

Richter added that he believed Coy had been drinking but never saw him drink that day. Coy had his back turned on Krempkau on the first shot, according to the witness, and was approximately eighteen feet away from the door. By the time Coy was struck by the third shot he was "five or six feet" from the south door.[19]

Richter also testified that Coy cursed Krempkau:[20] "He cursed him in English, but when he was going off he said some Spanish words."[21]

The district attorney cross-examined Richter and, through rapid-fire questions and differently worded statements, confused him sometimes to the point of contradicting his earlier story. The same was true when a bartender, Theodore Leonard, testified on Krempkau's behalf.[22] The first day of testimony ended at 5:00 P.M. with four witnesses being called.[23]

The proceedings were postponed the second day because one of Krempkau's attorneys was detained by another case in Austin.[24]

The third day was successful for Krempkau as the court released him on $5,000 bail. Providing sureties were Frank Beitel, August Santleman, Emil Niggil, John Loustannan, Henry Inselmann, and Paul Bergeron.[25]

Krempkau's counsel produced "a ferocious looking jack knife with Coy's initials engraved upon the handle, which it was said Coy had had in his hand when the shooting was done." Another witness testified that the knife had been taken away from Coy before the shooting started.[26]

District Attorney Paschal stated that he was satisfied with the recognizance bond and the conditions enabling Krempkau to be released.[27]

The 37th District Court ordered that case number 9314 of *The State of Texas v. Albert Krempkau* on Thursday, January 25, 1894, be continued by consent. Val Leonard, Henry Krempkau, and Charles Richter also appeared in court that day to notify the state that they would each be indebted to the state for $100 as witnesses in the Albert Krempkau case.[28]

Krempkau continued to work in the saloon. He never went to trial for Coy's murder. Charges against him were dismissed on Wednesday, February 7, 1900, because of his death.[29] He is in the county records for having paid a $150 state and $25 county poll tax for property on Houston and Laredo streets in 1898.

The newspaper stories do not agree on many of the basic facts, much less the supposition regarding the characters and the case.

Krempkau was quick with his temper. He was approximately thirty-five years old at the time of the shooting and was a brother-in-law of Sheriff McCall. Krempkau was single at the time of the shooting and had lived in San Antonio all of his life.

Coy was drunk, and he was cocky. He didn't think Krempkau would shoot. Krempkau had already missed one shot and Coy could have done anything, including charge his adversary and disengage the gun, if he had liked. The entire scene was a game for Coy. He had cheated death before and was confident he could do it again.

There were no other mentions of Coy killing a Trevino in Wilson County after the Butler feud or of the DeWitt County murder indictment. The reporting of such incidents wasn't accurate, and most records no longer exist. It was easy for policemen and sheriffs to tag a couple of more unsolved murders on a notorious killer such as Coy to clean their slate. It was also easy for rumors to turn into "fact."

San Antonio had just gone through an extremely violent period years earlier. It was difficult to be a decent and law-abiding citizen without being harassed and shot at, especially when the culprits were not even pursued or prosecuted. It was so bad that a group of citizens banded together to form a vigilante committee. The group was swift with the justice they carried out, which usually consisted of hanging from a tree.

It's amazing that Juan Coy was never the subject of the vigilante's justice.

The Wild West days were coming to an end and people were becoming more civilized. People complain today about the negative newspaper stories and the sad decay of society. They point to the better days of yesteryear, when morals and family values were high. But consider these stories from 1892 about the problems faced in "the good ol' days" more than 100 years ago.

Katie Coggsholl, twelve years old, committed suicide from opium,[30] and her stepfather, Ed Hawkins, attempted suicide by morphine the next day.[31]

The city government had its problems back then but of a different magnitude than today. It was reported on May 6, 1892, that city officers and employees were to be paid the next day for the first time in three months. Col. George W. Brackenridge advanced the city $80,000 to pay the salaries because the city treasury had no money.[32]

Baseball was having financial troubles, as reported in June 1892, with some teams not as prosperous as others.[33] Judge Adams ruled F. Barr, a barber, guilty for breaking the Sabbath. Barr was fined $10 and court costs for shaving men on the Sabbath, according to the July 27, 1892, *San Antonio Daily Express*.[34]

The main problem plaguing the San Antonio Police Department during the early 1892 period was an arson epidemic. Melissa Williams, a black thirteen-year-old girl, was sentenced on May 14, 1892, for setting fire to her employers' house.[35] The fires didn't end until Joe McDonald, seventeen years old, was captured Friday, July 22, and charged with three counts of arson and six of burglary. He was indicted, according to the October 6, 1892, *San Antonio Daily Express*, for eighteen counts of arson and burglary by theft.[36]

John Wesley Hardin, the state's most notorious and deadliest killer, was still in prison when Coy died. Hardin went to jail with more than forty notches on his gun, probably more than Juan Coy. Hardin was in prison from 1878 until 1894. He tried in vain to escape from prison but was betrayed each time by fellow prisoners. The son of a Methodist minister, Hardin eventually devoted his time to reading and became a lawyer before leaving prison. He was in El Paso in 1895 to try a case when Constable John Selman gunned Hardin down from behind.[37]

Despite roaming South Texas, albeit just a little north of Coy's territory in the same 1870s, Hardin was buried in El Paso. Some of Hardin's travels took him to Gonzales, Seguin, Kerrville, and Cuero. There have been unsuccessful attempts to return his body to the Gonzales area.

The times were changing in South Texas and the nation. Wide open prairies that provided endless grazing for cattle were now being shut off with barbed wire. Cattle drives were a thing of the past, giving way to transporting cattle by rail. Automobiles were next on the horizon, thanks to Henry Ford's mass production line in 1903. Air travel wasn't too far behind.

Butler continued his ranching business near Kenedy. He would sit on his large, expansive porch and watch the trains pass

William Butler could sit on the porch of his spacious home and watch the trains transport his cattle to market.

(Photo courtesy of Charlotte Nichols)

just a couple of hundred yards from his eight-room mansion.[38] It was the trains that would have passed through Helena which slowly deteriorated after Butler gave the land and money to move the rail line closer to Kenedy.

Butler would ride in "an old two-horse buggy that looked like it had been worn out years ago, and the harness was mostly chains, rawhide and wire. He had a young wooden-legged Negro to do the driving for him."[39] Friends and acquaintances would ask Butler for a loan, but the old gentleman would point to the pitiful condition of his buggy, complain that he couldn't afford a new buggy, and that would stop any requests.[40]

Butler helped organize the Karnes County National Bank in Karnes City in 1901 and served on its first board of directors. Sykes Butler was the bank's first president.[41] A bank statement of September 9, 1903, listed the resources at $96,098.63.[42] A year later, the two Butlers helped organize the First State Bank of Kenedy. The elder Butler was on the board of directors and Sykes was the first president.[43]

William Butler was a shrewd and careful businessman. He prospered greatly from the cattle industry, thanks to keeping up with the advances. He predicted, in his later years, that in time the government would own all the land in the United States through taxation.[44]

Butler was in failing health later in life, especially after his wife died on April 7, 1908. He still entertained and presided over gatherings of his large family. The July 11, 1911, edition of the *Kenedy Advance* reported that B. F. Burris from Cotulla was visiting relatives in the Kenedy area as a guest of his uncle, William G. Butler.[45]

At the time of his death, Butler owned approximately 75,000 acres of land and leased another 25,000 acres. He owned 10,000 head of cattle and 5,000 horses.[46]

William Green Butler died at his home, of natural causes, at 3:15 A.M. June 14, 1912, just six days before his seventy-eighth birthday. The funeral was at the family residence Saturday afternoon and was conducted by Rev. A. L. Ingram, pastor of the Baptist church in Kenedy.[47]

Butler was buried in the Butler Family Cemetery near Kenedy. Pallbearers were J. L. Brown, L. E. Bain, S. R. Franklin, J. W. Nichols, W. A. Teas, T. A. Miller, J. W. Ruckman, and H. W. Dailey.

Honorary pallbearers were J. M. Nichols, J. A. Martin, John Ruckman, W. J. Rutledge, D. A. T. Walton, and Walter P. Napier, Sr. Butler, who had been a member of the Masonic order since 1855, was buried with Masonic honors.⁴⁸ He was a member of the Kenedy Lodge No. 774 and earned as high as the Royal Arch Degree.⁴⁹ Butler is buried next to his wife, Adeline, who died in 1908 at the age of sixty-nine.

Butler's children buried at the family cemetery are: Emmett, who was shot to death in Helena in 1884; Newton, who died in 1895 at age thirty-six; Marion, who died after surviving just ten days; Sykes, who died in 1946; Cora Ann, who lived to the age of seventy-seven; Theodore Green Butler, who died in 1948 at the age of seventy-six; and William Green, Jr., who died just a year after his father at the age of thirty-seven.⁵⁰

William Butler had lived through the first transcontinental railroad, as well as the invention of the automobile and the airplane. The April 7, 1911, edition of *The Kenedy Advance* noted that "Dr. R. L. Hammack received a new five-passenger Ford automobile Wednesday, which brings the total for Karnes County to 62."⁵¹

Shootouts still occur in San Antonio saloons and convenience stores. It has become human nature for people to try to get the upper hand through violence, preferably with guns. Most arguments that end in shootings are started after the consumption of alcohol, a problem Juan Coy had in the 1800s.

Today very few people outside the Coy family have ever heard of Juan Coy. His actions and the fact that he worked both sides of the law make him an interesting character from the Wild West days. If he indeed killed as many as he claimed to have killed (thirty-three), today he would be considered a very serious threat to society, and he would have been severely punished. But he was out in the open and he was a lawman, which makes it almost sad that he wasn't killed in a more romantic fashion instead of being killed unarmed in a bar. It would have been more fitting if he had been killed in a wild exchange of gunfire.

The Shootout at the O.K. Corral claimed three lives on October 26, 1881, as compared to five deaths at the Daileyville Election Riot less than five years later. The Daileyville Election Riot lasted longer and involved more people than the shooting in Tombstone, Arizona, yet Daileyville no longer exists while Tombstone is a tourist attraction. There have been movies, books, and websites about the O.K. Corral, while Daileyville is virtually unknown even in South Texas.

Gone are the days of protection and the hired gun that Juan Coy supplied William Butler, who would bail him out of trouble. Gone also are the days of killing a minority or member of the lower class in society and not being prosecuted for it.

Or at least we try to think so.

Notes

Introduction

1. "Diary of Jesse Perez," The Center for American History (Austin, Texas: University of Texas at Austin), p. 18.
2. "A TRAGEDY. JUAN COY KILLED LAST NIGHT," *The Daily Light*, January 26, 1892, p. 1.
3. "Diary of Jesse Perez," p. 4.
4. James Kimmims Greer, *Colonel Jack Hays* (New York, New York: E. P. Dutton and Company, Inc., 1952), p. 63.
5. Arnoldo DeLeon, *The Tejano Community 1836-1900* (Albuquerque, New Mexico: University of New Mexico Press, 1982), p. 103.
6. "Diary of Jesse Perez," pp. 3-4.
7. Frederick Law Olmsted, *A Journey Through Texas* (Austin, Texas: University of Texas Press, 1857), p. 158.
8. Maxine Yeater Linder, "Wofford Crossing Road: The Autobiography of Maxine Yeater Linder of Kenedy, Karnes County, Texas," Volume 1 (Private publication, 1994), p. 100.
9. "A TRAGEDY. JUAN COY KILLED LAST NIGHT," *The Daily Light*, January 26, 1892, p. 1.
10. *Ibid.*
11. Karnes County Historical Society, "Welcome to Old Helena."
12. Doctor Joseph Jones' statement on Juan Coy's pension claim, National Archives and Records Administration.
13. Elton Cude, *The Free and Wild Dukedom of Bexar* (San Antonio, Texas: Munguia Printers, 1978), p. 93.
14. *Ibid.*

Chapter One

1. *The Mexican Texans* (San Antonio, Texas: The University of Texas Institute of Texan Cultures, 1975), p. 3.
2. *Ibid.*
3. "Aged Mexican's Death Recalls Events of Early Days in Karnes Section," *Kenedy Advance*, January 16, 1936.

4. *Ibid.*
5. *Ibid.*
6. *Ibid.*
7. *Ibid.*
8. "Diary of Jesse Perez," p. 3.
9. *San Antonio Daily Herald,* June 27, 1878, p. 4.
10. *Ibid.,* June 11, 1878, p. 4.
11. "Aged Mexican's Death Recalls Events of Early Days in Karnes Section."
12. T. Lindsay Baker, *The Polish Texans* (San Antonio, Texas: The University of Texas Institute of Texan Cultures, 1982), p. 88.
13. *Ibid.*
14. *Ibid.*
15. *Ibid.*
16. Hedwig Krell Didear, *A History of Karnes County and Old Helena* (Austin, Texas: San Felipe Press, 1969), p. 29.
17. *The Polish Texans,* p. 27.
18. George W. Saunders, *The Trail Drivers of Texas* (New York: Lamar and Barton, 1924), p. 715.
19. *Ibid.*
20. Heep Plummer, "The man who didn't kill the town that killed his boy," *Karnes Citation-Kenedy Advance-Times,* December 16, 1987, p. 6.
21. Maxine Yeater Linder, "Wofford Crossing Road: Autobiography of Maxine Yeater Linder of Kenedy, Karnes County, Texas," Volume 1 (Private publication, 1994), p. 87.

Chapter Two
1. Letter from Texas Department of Criminal Justice, Institutional Division, August 15, 1997.
2. *The Daily Light,* January 26, 1892, p. 1.
3. Frederick Charles Chabot, *With the Makers of San Antonio* (San Antonio, Texas: Artes Graficas, 1937), p. 76.
4. *San Antonio Daily Express,* January 19, 1891, p. 6.
5. Joseph Milton Nance, *Attack and Counterattack* (Austin, Texas: University of Texas Press, 1964), p. 16.
6. Greer, *Colonel Jack Hays,* p. 263.
7. Family history records courtesy of Los Bexarenos.
8. Chabot, *With the Makers of San Antonio,* p. 77.
9. Genealogical records compiled by Charlotte Nichols, Kenedy, Texas, library.
10. *Ibid.*
11. *Ibid.*
12. Anne Dingus, ed., *The Book of Texas Lists!!* (Austin, Texas: Texas Monthly Press, 1981), p. 65.
13. Gra'Delle Duncan, *Texas Tough—Dangerous Men in Dangerous Times* (Austin, Texas: Eakin Press, 1990), p. 37.
14. Duncan, *The Book of Texas Lists!!,* p. 23.
15. Olmsted, *A Journey Through Texas,* p. 472.

16. Ron Tyler, ed., *The New Handbook of Texas* (Austin, Texas: The Texas State Historical Association, 1996), p. 866.
17. *Ibid.*
18. "Report of the Adjutant General of the State of Texas for the Year 1873." (Austin, Texas: Cardwell & Walker Printers, 1874), p. 66.
19. Jack Maguire, *Texas: Amazing But True* (Austin, Texas: Eakin Press, 1984), p. 105.
20. Union Muster Roll, National Archives and Records Administration.
21. *Ibid.*
22. Webb Garrison, *A Treasury of Texas Tales* (Nashville, Tennessee: Rutledge Hill Press, 1997), p. 97.
23. *Ibid.*, p. 98.
24. *Ibid.*, p. 101.
25. Union Muster Roll.
26. *History of Southwest Texas* (Lewis Publishing Company, 1907), p. 333.
27. *Ibid.*
28. *Ibid.*
29. "The man who didn't kill the town that killed his boy," p. 6.
30. *History of Southwest Texas*, p. 333.
31. *Ibid.*
32. "Builders of Texas Collection to 1942," The Texas State Library and Archives, compiled by Charlotte Nichols, p. 8.
33. *Ibid.*
34. *Ibid.*
35. *Ibid.*, p. 8B.
36. *Ibid.*
37. Saunders, *The Trail Drivers of Texas*, p. 716.
38. Interview with Robert Thonhoff.
39. "The man who didn't kill the town that killed his boy," p. 6.
40. *Ibid.*
41. Saunders, *The Trail Drivers of Texas*, p. 716.
42. *Ibid.*, p. 717.
43. *Ibid.*
44. Karnes County 1880 Census, Enumeration District Number 8.
45. Dr. Joseph Jones' statement on Juan Coy's pension claim, National Archives and Records Administration.
46. *Ibid.*
47. Saunders, *The Trail Drivers of Texas*, p. 717.
48. *Ibid.*
49. *Ibid.*
50. Dingus, ed., *The Book of Texas Lists!!*, p. 30.
51. Notes from Karnes County docket minutes, 1885.

Chapter Three

1. William L. Roper, "Rendezvous with Vengeance," *Texas Parade,* June 1954, p. 43.
2. *Ibid.*

3. *Ibid.*
4. *Ibid.*
5. *Ibid.*
6. O. C. Fisher, *King Fisher: His Life and Times* (Norman, Oklahoma, University of Oklahoma Press, 1966), p. 125.
7. Roper, "Rendezvous with Vengeance," p. 44.
8. Texas Folklore, *San Antonio Express-News*, February 16, 1997, p. 24A.
9. Roper, "Rendezvous with Vengeance," p. 44.
10. *Ibid.*
11. *Ibid.*
12. *Ibid.*
13. *Ibid.*
14. *Ibid.*
15. *Ibid*, p. 45.
16. *Ibid.*
17. *Ibid.*
18. *Ibid*, p. 47.
19. *Ibid.*
20. *Ibid.*
21. Cude, *The Free and Wild Dukedom of Bexar*, p. 117.
22. O. C. Fisher, *King Fisher: His Life and Times*, p. 125.
23. Roper, "Rendezvous with Vengeance," p. 44.
24. O. C. Fisher, *King Fisher: His Life and Times*, p. 125.
25. Roper, "Rendezvous with Vengeance," p. 44.
26. Cude, *The Free and Wild Dukedom of Bexar*, p. 117.
27. Billy Mac Jones, *The Search for Maturity* (Austin, Texas: Steck-Vaughn Company, 1965), p. 11.
28. James L. Haley, *Texas, An Album of History* (Garden City, NY: Doubleday and Company, Inc., 1985), p. 244.
29. Jones, Search for Maturity, p. 12.
30. DeLeon, *The Tejano Community 1836-1900*, p. 104.
31. Walter P. Webb, *The Texas Rangers* (Austin, Texas: University of Texas Press, 1965), p. 287.
32. Tyler, ed., *The New Handbook of Texas*, p. 1011.
33. *Ibid.*
34. Webb, *The Texas Rangers*, p. 286.
35. *Ibid.*, p. 287.
36. T. R. Fehrenbach, *Lone Star* (New York: American Legacy Press, 1983), p. 559.
37. Tyler, ed., *The New Handbook of Texas*, p. 1011.

Chapter Four
1. Dingus, ed., *The Book of Texas Lists!!*, p. 77.
2. Duncan, *Texas Tough—Dangerous Men in Dangerous Times*, p. 80.
3. *Ibid.*
4. *Ibid.*, p. 81.
5. "Diary of Jesse Perez," p. 18.
6. *Ibid.*, p. 17.

7. *Ibid.*, p. 18.
8. *Ibid.*
9. *Ibid.*
10. *San Antonio Daily Herald,* June 25, 1878, Vol. 21, No. 157, p. 6.
11. *Ibid.*, June 11, 1878, Vol. 21, No. 155, p. 4.
12. *Ibid.*, June 12, 1878, Vol. 21, No. 156, p. 4.
13. *Ibid.*, June 22, 1878, Vol. 21, No. 155, p. 4.
14. *Ibid.*
15. *San Antonio Daily Herald,* June 25, 1878, Vol. 21, No. 157, p. 6.
16. *Ibid.*
17. *Ibid.*
18. *San Antonio Daily Herald,* June 28, 1878, p. 4.
19. Letter from Texas Department of Criminal Justice.
20. "Diary of Jesse Perez," p. 18.
21. Dingus, ed., *The Book of Texas Lists!!,* p. 96.
22. John Wesley Hardin, *The Life of John Wesley Hardin as Written by Himself* (Norman, Oklahoma: University of Oklahoma Press, 1961), p. xii.
23. Dingus, ed., *The Book of Texas Lists!!,* p. 21.
24. *Ibid.*, p. 96.
25. *Ibid.*
26. *San Antonio Daily Herald,* June 27, 1878, p. 4.
27. "Recorder's Court," *San Antonio Daily Light,* July 3, 1886, p. 1.
28. *Ibid.*

Chapter Five
1. "The man who didn't kill the town that killed his boy," p. 6.
2. Archie B. Ammons, *Notes on Karnes County History,* p. 2.
3. Linder, "Wofford Crossing Road," p. 93.
4. "The man who didn't kill the town that killed his boy," p. 6.
5. *Ibid.*
6. Baker, *The Polish Texans,* p. 88.
7. Joe Tom Davis, *Historic Towns of Texas* (Austin, Texas: Eakin Press, 1992) p. 230.
8. Karnes County Historical Society, "Welcome to Old Helena."
9. "RESULT OF A FEUD: MORTAL COMBAT ON THE STREETS OF HELENA," *The Daily Express,* December 30, 1884.
10. "THE KARNES AFFRAY: How the Two Men Met Their Deaths," *The Daily Express,* December 31, 1884.
11. *Ibid.*
12. Linder, "Wofford Crossing Road," p. 93.
13. "RESULT OF A FEUD."
14. *Ibid.*
15. Linder, "Wofford Crossing Road," p. 95.
16. *Ibid.*
17. *Ibid.*, p. 96.
18. *Ibid.*
19. *Ibid.*

20. *Ibid.*
21. *Ibid.*
22. *Ibid.*
23. *Ibid.*
24. *Ibid.*, p. 97.
25. *Ibid.*
26. Ammons, "Notes on Karnes County," p. 1.
27. "THE KARNES AFFRAY."
28. *Ibid.*
29. *Ibid.*
30. Davis, *Historic Towns of Texas*, p. 230.
31. *Ibid.*
32. *Ibid.*
33. *Ibid.*
34. *Ibid.*
35. *Ibid.*, p. 231.
36. *Ibid.*
37. Karnes County Historical Society, "Welcome to Old Helena."
38. "THE KARNES AFFRAY."
39. "RESULT OF A FEUD."
40. *Ibid.*
41. *Ibid.*
42. *Ibid.*
43. "The man who didn't kill the town that killed his boy."
44. "THE KARNES AFFRAY."
45. *Ibid.*
46. *Ibid.*
47. *Ibid.*
48. "The man who didn't kill the town that killed his boy."
49. *Ibid.*
50. 1880 Karnes County Census.
51. Saunders, *The Trail Drivers of Texas*, p. 716.
52. 1880 Karnes County Census.
53. Karnes County Historical Society, "Welcome to Old Helena."
54. Davis, *Historic Towns of Texas*, p. 228.
55. *Ibid.*, p. 229.
56. Karnes County Historical Society, "Welcome to Old Helena."
57. *Ibid.*
58. Davis, *Historic Towns of Texas*, p. 231.
59. *Ibid.*
60. *Ibid.*
61. *Ibid.*
62. *Ibid.*

Chapter Six

1. *San Antonio Daily Light,* July 15, 1886, p. 1. Donald Everett, *San Antonio Legacy* (San Antonio, Texas: Trinity University Press, 1979), p. 33.

2. "Diary of Jesse Perez," p. 4.
3. *Ibid.*, p. 5.
4. *Ibid.*
5. *Ibid.*
6. *Ibid.*, p. 6.
7. *Ibid.*
8. *Ibid.*, p. 7.
9. *Ibid.*
10. *Ibid.*, p. 8.
11. *Ibid.*
12. *Ibid.*
13. *Ibid.*, p. 9.
14. *Ibid.*
15. *Ibid.*
16. *Ibid.*
17. *Ibid.*
18. *Ibid.*
19. *Ibid.*, p. 10.
20. *Ibid.*
21. *Ibid.*
22. *Ibid.*
23. *Ibid.*, p. 11.
24. *Ibid.*
25. *Ibid.*
26. *Ibid.*

Chapter Seven
1. Mark Louis Rybczyk, *San Antonio Uncovered* (Plano, Texas: Wordware Publishing, Inc., 1992), p. 10.
2. DeLeon, *The Tejano Community 1836-1900*, p. 107.
3. *Ibid.*
4. "Train Boarded—By Armed Men and Two Supposed Mexican Horse Thieves Shot and Killed," *San Antonio Daily Light*, June 29, 1886, p. 1.
5. *Ibid.*
6. *Ibid.*
7. "Aransas Pass Railway Notes," *San Antonio Daily Light*, June 30, 1886, p. 1.
8. Davis, *Historic Towns of Texas*, p. 231.
9. Notes from Karnes County book of minutes.
10. *Ibid.*
11. San Antonio Sporting District booklet.
12. "Recorder's Court," *San Antonio Daily Light*, June 29, 1886, p. 4.
13. *Ibid.*
14. "Recorder's Court," *San Antonio Daily Light*, July 3, 1886, p.1.
15. *Ibid.*

Chapter Eight
1. Testimony of Ildefonso Coy in hearing on September 6, 1886, shooting.

2. *Ibid.*
3. "Floresville Killing," *San Antonio Daily Light,* June 29, 1886, p. 1.
4. *Ibid.*
5. *Ibid.*
6. "Floresville Topics," *San Antonio Daily Light,* July 1, 1886, p. 1.
7. Testimony of Ildefonso Coy.
8. *Ibid.*
9. "Personal," *San Antonio Daily Light,* July 6, 1886, p. 4.
10. Testimony of Ildefonso Coy.

Chapter Nine
1. Linder, "Wofford Crossing Road," p. 98.
2. *Ibid.*, p. 100.
3. Brownson Malsch, *Indianola: The Mother of Western Texas* (Austin, Texas: State House Press, 1988), p. 265.
4. *San Antonio Daily Light,* July 15 1886, p. 1.
5. Testimony of Andy Nichols given before Jury of Inquest on September 6, 1886, shooting.
6. Testimony of Will Harrold given before Jury of Inquest on September 6, 1886, shooting.
7. Testimony of Eli Harrold given before Jury of Inquest on September 6, 1886, shooting.
8. Testimony of Eli Harrold.
9. Testimony of Will Harrold, Eli Harrold, and John Trimble.
10. Testimony of Eli Harrold.
11. Testimony of Jack Pullin given before Jury of Inquest on September 6, 1886, shooting.
12. Testimony of Eli Harrold.
13. Testimony of M. M. Mayfield given before Jury of Inquest on September 6, 1886, shooting.
14. Testimony of John Shuler given before Jury of Inquest on September 6, 1886, shooting.
15. Testimony of Eli Harrold.
16. Testimony of Will Harrold.
17. Testimony of Eli Harrold.
18. *Ibid.*
19. *Ibid.*
20. Testimony of Will Harrold.
21. Testimony of Hugh Pace given before Jury of Inquest on September 6, 1886, shooting.
22. Linder, "Wofford Crossing Road," p. 100.
23. "The Daileyville Killing," *San Antonio Daily Express,* September 16, 1886.
24. Testimony of Hugh Pace.
25. Testimony of Will Harrold.
26. Testimony of F. R. Graves given before Jury of Inquest on September 6, 1886, shooting.
27. *Ibid.*

28. Testimony of Will Harrold.
29. Testimony of John L. Sullivan given before Jury of Inquest on September 6, 1886, shooting.
30. Testimony of P. B. Butler given before Jury of Inquest on September 6, 1886, shooting.
31. Linder, "Wofford Crossing Road," p. 101.
32. Testimony of Will Harrold.
33. *Ibid.*
34. Testimony of John L. Sullivan.
35. Linder, "Wofford Crossing Road," p. 101.
36. *Ibid.*
37. "The man who didn't kill the town that killed his boy."
38. Linder, "Wofford Crossing Road," p. 101.
39. "The Daileyville Killing."
40. *Ibid.*
41. Testimony of John Trimble.
42. *Ibid.*
43. "The Daileyville Killing."
44. "The Karnes County Tragedy," *San Antonio Daily Express,* September 8, 1886, p. 4.
45. Testimony of Charles Coleman given before Jury of Inquest on September 6, 1886, shooting.
46. *Ibid.*
47. Testimony of Sam Dailey given before Jury of Inquest on September 6, 1886, shooting.
48. *Ibid.*
49. Linder, "Wofford Crossing Road," p. 102.
50. *Ibid.*
51. *Ibid.*, p. 109.
52. Testimony of Jack Pullin.
53. *Ibid.*
54. *Ibid.*
55. Testimony of Andy Nichols.
56. *Ibid.*
57. Testimony of Jack Pullin.
58. Testimony of Dr. S. G. Dailey given before Jury of Inquest on September 6, 1886, shooting.
59. Testimony of Jack Pullin.
60. Testimony of Cebelo Sanchez given before Jury of Inquest on September 6, 1886, shooting.
61. *Ibid.*
62. Testimony of Dr. S. G. Dailey.
63. Testimony of Sam Dailey given before Jury of Inquest on September 6, 1886, shooting.
64. *Ibid.*
65. Testimony of Dr. S.G. Dailey.
66. *Ibid.*

67. *Ibid.*
68. *Ibid.*
69. "The Daileyville Killing."
70. *Ibid.*
71. *Ibid.*

Chapter Ten
1. Testimony given before Jury of Inquest.
2. Testimony of Will Harrold.
3. Testimony of John Trimble.
4. *San Antonio Light,* September 7, 1886.
5. Testimony of F. R. Graves.
6. *Ibid.*
7. Testimony of Dr. S. G. Dailey.
8. Testimony of F. R. Graves.
9. Testimony of William G. Butler given before Jury of Inquest on September 6, 1886, shooting.
10. *Ibid.*
11. "Tragedy in Karnes County," *Victoria Advocate,* September 11, 1886, p. 1.
12. "Diary of Jesse Perez," p. 11.
13. *Ibid.*
14. *Victoria Advocate,* September 18, 1886, p. 1.
15. *Ibid.*
16. "Opinion of a San Antonio Lawyer on its Lawlessness," *San Antonio Daily Express,* September 17, 1886, p. 5.
17. "Defends his County," *San Antonio Daily Express,* September 22, 1886, p. 7.
18. *Ibid.*
19. *Ibid.*
20. *Ibid.*
21. "Diary of Jesse Perez," p. 12.
22. *Ibid.*
23. *Ibid.*
24. "Coy's Arrest," *San Antonio Daily Express,* October 12, 1886, p. 4.
25. "Diary of Jesse Perez," p. 12.
26. "Coy's Arrest," p. 4.
27. *Ibid.*
28. *Ibid.*
29. Karnes County docket minutes.
30. *Ibid.*
31. "A Bad Mexican," *San Antonio Daily Express,* October 20, 1886, p. 8.
32. *Ibid.*
33. "Notes on Karnes County History," p. 6.
34. *Ibid.*
35. "The Daileyville Killing," *San Antonio Daily Express,* October 21, 1886, p. 5.
36. "Notes on Karnes County History," p. 6.
37. "The Daileyville Killing."

38. *Ibid.*
39. *San Antonio Daily Express,* December 1, 1886, p. 3.
40. *Ibid.,* December 8, 1886, p. 1.
41. "News from Laredo," *San Antonio Daily Express,* December 14, 1886, p. 2.
42. "The Karnes County Cases," *San Antonio Daily Express,* December 12, 1886, p. 4.
43. *Ibid.*
44. *Ibid.*
45. *Ibid.*
46. Karnes County docket minutes.
47. *Ibid.*
48. *Ibid.*
49. *Ibid.*
50. Linder, "Wofford Crossing Road," p. 103.
51. Karnes County docket minutes.
52. *Ibid.*
53. *Ibid.*
54. "Floresville Chronicles," *San Antonio Daily Express,* June 15, 1887, p. 2.
55. *Ibid.*
56. *Ibid.*
57. *Ibid.*
58. *Ibid.,* June 18, 1886, p. 2.
59. *Ibid.*
60. *Ibid.,* June 22, 1887, p. 2.
61. *Ibid.*
62. Karnes County docket minutes.
63. "Notes on Karnes County History," p. 3.
64. Linder, "Wofford Crossing Road," p. 103.
65. *Ibid.,* p. 104.
66. *Ibid.*
67. "Notes on Karnes County History," p. 5.

Chapter Eleven
1. Marriage certificate, San Antonio Archdiocese records.
2. Baptism record, San Antonio Archdiocese records.
3. Ibid.
4. Ibid.
5. Jacoba Coy's "Declaration for Widow's Pension," National Archives and Records Administration.
6. Copy of birth certificate of Jacoba Reyes.
7. Copy of birth certificate of Alejos Coy.

Chapter Thirteen
1. Rybczyk, *San Antonio Uncovered,* p. 268.
2. Dr. Joseph Jones' statement on Juan Coy's pension claim, National Archives and Records Administration.
3. General Affidavit on Juan Coy's pension claim, National Archives and Records Administration.

4. Dr. Joseph Jones' statement on Juan Coy's pension claim, National Archives and Records Administration.
5. Juan Coy's "Declaration For Invalid Pension," National Archives and Records Administration.

Chapter Fourteen
1. "Diary of Jesse Perez," p. 12.
2. *Ibid.*
3. *Ibid.*, p. 13.
4. *Ibid.*
5. *Ibid.*, p. 14.
6. *Ibid.*
7. *Ibid.*, p. 15.
8. *Ibid.*
9. *Ibid.*
10. *Ibid.*
11. *Ibid.*
12. *Ibid.*, p. 16.
13. *Ibid.*
14. *Ibid.*
15. *Ibid.*
16. *Ibid.*
17. "A Tragedy," *The Daily Light,* January 26, 1892, p. 1.
18. *Ibid.*
19. "Diary of Jesse Perez," p. 16.
20. "A Tragedy," *The Daily Light.*
21. *Ibid.*
22. "He Ended Coy's Career," *San Antonio Daily Express,* January 26, 1892, p. 3.
23. "A Tragedy," *The Daily Light.*
24. *Ibid.*
25. *Ibid.*
26. *Ibid.*
27. *Ibid.*
28. *Ibid.*
29. "Diary of Jesse Perez," p. 17.
30. "He Ended Coy's Career," *San Antonio Daily Express,* January 26, 1892, p. 3.
31. "A Tragedy," *The Daily Light.*
32. "He Ended Coy's Career," *San Antonio Daily Express,* January 26, 1892, p. 3.
33. *Ibid.*
34. *Ibid.*
35. *Ibid.*
36. *Ibid.*
37. "Diary of Jesse Perez," p. 17.
38. "Floresville Chronicles," *San Antonio Daily Express,* January 30, 1892, p. 2.

39. *Ibid.*
40. *San Antonio Daily Express,* January 31, 1892, p. 2.
41. Wedding certificate of Jacoba De Los Reyes.
42. "Widow's Pension," National Archives and Records Administration.
43. Coy Family Archives.

Chapter Fifteen
1. "Juan Coy Shot," *New York Times,* January 26, 1892, p. 3.
2. *Ibid.*
3. *Ibid.*
4. *Ibid.*
5. *Ibid.*
6. *Ibid.*
7. "A Tragedy," *The Daily Light.*
8. *San Antonio Daily Express,* January 28, 1892, p. 4.
9. *Ibid.*
10. *Ibid.,* January 31, 1892, p. 2.
11. *Ibid.,* February 1, 1892, p. 5.
12. "Krempkau in Court," *San Antonio Daily Express,* February 13, 1892, p. 5.
13. *Ibid.,* February 14, 1892, p. 6.
14. *Ibid.*
15. *Ibid.*
16. *Ibid.*
17. *Ibid.*
18. *Ibid.*
19. *Ibid.*
20. *Ibid.*
21. *Ibid.*
22. *Ibid.*
23. *Ibid.*
24. "Result Not Reached," *San Antonio Daily Express,* February 19, 1892, p. 8.
25. "Krempkau Out On Bail," *San Antonio Daily Express,* February 25, 1892, p. 5.
26. *Ibid.*
27. *Ibid.*
28. Bexar County docket minutes, Case No. 9314.
29. *Ibid.*
30. *San Antonio Daily Express,* May 2, 1892.
31. *Ibid.,* May 3, 1892.
32. *Ibid.,* May 6, 1892.
33. *Ibid.,* June 27, 1892.
34. *Ibid.,* July 27, 1892.
35. *Ibid.,* May 14, 1892.
36. *Ibid.,* July 24, 1892.
37. Dingus, ed., *The Book of Texas Lists!!,* p. 96.
38. Linder, "Wofford Crossing Road," p. 94.
39. "Historical Facts and People of Karnes County," *The Kenedy Advance,* July 17, 1958, p. 3.

40. *Ibid.*
41. "Builders of Texas Collection to 1942," p. 4A.
42. Karnes County National Bank statement.
43. "Builders of Texas Collection to 1942," p. 4A.
44. *Ibid.*, p. 5.
45. *The Kenedy Advance,* July 21, 1911, Vol. 16, No. 19, p. 5.
46. "Builders of Texas Collection to 1942," p. 4A.
47. *Ibid.*
48. *Ibid.*
49. *History of Southwest Texas,* p. 334.
50. Genealogical records compiled by Charlotte Nichols.
51. "Another Auto for Kenedy," *The Kenedy Advance,* April 17, 1911, p. 8.

Bibliography

"A Bad Mexican." *San Antonio Daily Express.* October 20, 1886.
"A TRAGEDY. JUAN COY KILLED LAST NIGHT." *The Daily Light.* January 26, 1892.
"Aged Mexican's Death Recalls Events of Early Days in Karnes Section." *Kenedy Advance,* January 16, 1936.
Baker, Lindsay T. *The Polish Texans.* San Antonio, Texas: The University of Texas Institute of Texan Cultures, 1982.
Baptism records, courtesy of the Catholic Archives of San Antonio.
Bexar County docket minutes, Case No. 9314.
Copy of Jacoba Reyes birth certificate.
Copy of Alejos Coy birth certificate.
Coy Family Archives.
"Coy's Arrest." *San Antonio Daily Express.* September 22, 1886.
Cude, Elton. *The Free and Wild Dukedom of Bexar.* San Antonio, Texas: Munguia Printers, 1978.
"The Daileyville Killing." *San Antonio Daily Express.* September 16, 1886, and October 21, 1886.
Davis, Joe Tom. *Historic Towns of Texas, Vol. I.* Austin, Texas: Eakin Press, 1992.
"Defends his County." *San Antonio Daily Express.* September 22, 1886.
DeLeon, Arnoldo. *The Tejano Community 1836-1900.* Albuquerque, New Mexico: University of New Mexico Press, 1982.
"Diary of Jesse Perez." The Center for American History, The University of Texas at Austin.
Dingus, Anne (editor). *The Book of Texas Lists!!* Austin, Texas: Texas Monthly Press, 1981.
Duncan, Gra'Delle. *Texas Tough—Dangerous Men in Dangerous Times.* Austin, Texas: Eakin Press, 1990.
Fehrenbach, T. R. *Lone Star.* New York, New York: American Legacy Press, 1983.
Fisher, O. C. *King Fisher: His Life and Times.* Norman, Oklahoma: University of Oklahoma Press, 1966.
"Floresville Chronicles." *San Antonio Daily Express.* June 15, 1886; June 18, 1886; June 22, 1887; January 30, 1892.

Garrison, Webb. *A Treasury of Texas Tales.* Nashville, Tennessee: Rutledge Hill Press, 1997.
Haley, James L. *Texas: An Album of History.* Garden City, New York: Doubleday and Company, Inc., 1985.
Hardin, John Wesley. *The Life of John Wesley Hardin as Written by Himself.* Norman, Oklahoma: University of Oklahoma Press, 1961.
"He Ended Coy's Career." *San Antonio Daily Express.* January 26, 1892.
History of the Southwest. Lewis Publishing, 1907.
Jones, Billy Mac. *The Search for Maturity.* Austin, Texas: Steck-Vaughn Company, 1965.
"Juan Coy Shot." *New York Times.* January 26, 1892.
"THE KARNES AFFRAY." *The Daily Express.* December 31, 1884.
"The Karnes County Cases." *San Antonio Daily Express.* December 12, 1886.
Karnes County docket minutes, 1885.
Karnes County 1880 Census, Enumeration District Number 8.
Karnes County Historical Society. "Welcome to Old Helena."
"The Karnes County Tragedy." *San Antonio Daily Express.* September 8, 1886.
"Krempkau in Court." *San Antonio Daily Express.* February 13, 1892; February 14, 1892.
"Krempkau Out On Bail." *San Antonio Daily Express.* February 25, 1892.
Linder, Maxine Yeater. "Wofford Crossing Road: The Autobiography of Maxine Yeater Linder of Kenedy, Karnes County, Texas." Volume 1. Private publication: 1994.
Los Bexarenos family records.
Maguire, Jack. *Texas: Amazing but True.* Austin, Texas: Eakin Press, 1984.
Marriage records, Catholic Archives of San Antonio.
The Mexican Texans. San Antonio, Texas: The University of Texas Institute of Texan Cultures, 1975.
Military records of William G. Butler, National Archives and Records Administration.
Military and pension records of Juan Coy, National Archives and Records Administration.
"News from Laredo." *San Antonio Daily Express.* December 14, 1886.
Olmsted, Frederick Law. *A Journey Through Texas.* Austin, Texas: University of Texas Press, 1857.
"Opinion of a San Antonio Lawyer on its Lawlessness." *San Antonio Daily Express.* September 17, 1886.
Plummer, Heep. "The man who didn't kill the town that killed his boy." *Karnes Citation-Kenedy Advance-Times.* December 16, 1987.
"Result Not Reached." *San Antonio Daily Express.* February 19, 1892.
"RESULT OF A FEUD. MORTAL COMBAT ON THE STREETS OF HELENA." *The Daily Express.* December 30, 1884.
Roper, William L. "Rendezvous with Vengeance." *Texas Parade.* June 1954.
Rybczyk, Mark Louis. *San Antonio Uncovered.* Plano, Texas: Wordware Publishing Inc., 1992.
San Antonio Daily Express. December 1, 1886; December 8, 1886; January 28, 1892; January 31, 1892; February 1, 1892; May 2, 1892; May 3, 1892; May 6, 1892; May 14, 1892; June 27, 1892; July 24, 1892; July 27, 1892.

San Antonio Express-News, February 16, 1997.
San Antonio Sporting District booklet.
Saunders, George W. *The Trail Drivers of Texas.* Lamar and Barton, 1924.
Testimony of P. B. Butler. September 6, 1886.
Testimony of William G. Butler. September 6, 1886.
Testimony of Ildefonso Coy. September 6, 1886.
Testimony of Charles Coleman. September 6, 1886.
Testimony of Dr. S. G. Dailey. September 6, 1886.
Testimony of Sam Dailey. September 6, 1886.
Testimony of F. R. Graves. September 6, 1886.
Testimony of Eli Harrold. September 6, 1886.
Testimony of Will Harrold. September 6, 1886.
Testimony of M.M. Mayfield. September 6, 1886.
Testimony of Andy Nichols. September 6, 1886.
Testimony of John Pace. September 6, 1886.
Testimony of Jack Pullin. September 6, 1886.
Testimony of Cebelo Sanchez. September 6, 1886.
Testimony of John Shuler. September 6, 1886.
Testimony of John L. Sullivan. September 6, 1886.
Testimony of John Trimble. September 6, 1886.
Thonhoff, Robert. Interview with author.
"Tragedy in Karnes County." *Victoria Advocate.* September 11, 1886.
Victoria Advocate. September 18, 1886.
Webb, Walter P. *The Texas Rangers.* Austin, Texas: University of Texas Press, 1965.

Index

• A •

Abilene, Kansas, 31, 32, 33, 54, 59
Adams, Anton, 134, 135, 141, 144
Alamita, 51
Alamo, xi, 73, 108, 122-123
Alamo, Battle of the, 2, 114-115, 122
Amarillo, Texas, 18, 33, 58
American Hotel, 43
Ammons, Jeff, 78
Appleville, 19
Arkansas Post, Battle of, 13
Atascosa County, xii, 1, 6, 74, 137
Atascosa Creek, 6
Austin, Stephen F., 74
Austin, Texas, 22, 24, 31, 78, 95

• B •

Bailey, Jack, 76, 77, 82, 83, 85, 86, 89, 90, 91, 99
Bain, L. E., 146
Bandera, 14
barbed wire, 59, 144
Barefield, Vivvy, 86
Barr, F., 144
Bass, Sam, xii, 37
Bastrop County, 137
Baton Rouge, Louisiana, 9
Beeville, 70
Beitel, Frank, 142
Bella Union Theater, 128, 134
Bergeron, Paul, 142
Bergstrom, Louis, 36
Bexar County, 1, 36, 141
Bexar County Courthouse, 108
Billy the Kid, xii
Binney, H., 36
Blair, Deputy Sheriff, 89
Booker, William, 36
Booth, John Wilkes, 38
Bowie, Jim, 122
Brackenridge, George W., 144
Brackenridge, Henry, 36
Brady, John, 18
Branch, Claud, 118
Brazos Santiago Island, Texas, 9
Brooklyn Bridge, 40
Brown, J. L., 146
Brown, L. H., 100
Brownsville, 33
Bull's Head Saloon, 31
Burges, W. H., 100
Burris, Adeline Riggs, 7
Burris, B. F., 146
Burris, Benjamin, 7
Burris, Jackson, 117
Burris, Susan Riggs, 7
Butler, Adeline, 7, 15, 41, 48, 50, 106, 112, 136, 146, 147
Butler, Burnell, 5
Butler, Cora, 8, 51, 147
Butler, D. B., 91, 99
Butler, Daniel, 96
Butler, Effie May, 50
Butler, Emmett, 8, 41, 79, 95, 104, 115, 147

Butler, Fayette, 18
Butler, Helen Adeline, 7, 51
Butler, Louissa M., 7, 51
Butler, M. L., 97
Butler, Marion, 8, 147
Butler, Mary A., 50
Butler, Newton G., 7, 50, 81, 82, 85, 91, 93, 147
Butler, P. B., 83, 97, 99
Butler, Pleas, 18, 44, 81
Butler, Robert, 18
Butler, Sallie, 5
Butler, Sykes Charles, 8, 51, 63, 64, 81, 82, 83, 91, 97, 99, 100, 102, 126, 146, 147
Butler, Theodore Green, 8, 51, 147
Butler, Wash, 18, 50
Butler, William Green, xii, 3, 5, 8-9, 13-17, 18, 33, 39, 41, 45-46, 51, 54, 58-59, 61, 63, 64, 65, 69, 70-72, 74, 78, 80, 81, 85, 89, 91, 92, 93, 94, 97, 98-99, 99-102, 104, 106, 109, 110, 112, 115-118, 121, 125-126, 136, 145-147
Butler, William Green "Hemis," Jr., 8, 51, 147
Butler, Woodward, 5
Butler-Elder Feud, 92
Butler family, x, xii, 5, 7, 16, 18-19, 39, 50-51, 62, 71, 73, 76, 79, 91, 94, 103, 106, 107, 112, 113, 115
Butler Family Cemetery, 146
Butler House, 43

• C •

Cadillac, 114
Calderon, Guadalupe, 6
Calvo, Father, 103
Canary Islanders, 1
Cantu, Luciano, 36, 135
Carhart, A., 36
Carpetbaggers, 17
Carter, 13
Carver-Mayfield store, 56
Cassiano, Jose, 36
Cassidy, Butch, xii
Castroville, 32
cattle rustling, 13-16
Chicago, Illinois, 40

Choate, Monroe, 85, 86
Civil War, 8-9, 14, 16, 17, 32, 52, 59, 68, 72, 75, 122, 123
Cline Station, 70
Cody, Buffalo Bill, 40
Coggsholl, Katie, 144
Coleman, Charles, 81, 86
Comanches, 7
Conquista, 3
Cooper, John, 50
Corpus Christi, Texas, 1, 70
Corpus Christi Raid, xi
Cortina, Juan Nepomuceno "Cheno," 33
Corwin, Sheriff, 36
Coy, Alejos (son of Juan II), 137, 138
Coy, Alejos (son of Juan and Jacoba), 106-107, 121, 129, 137
Coy, Alejos (son of Juan and Manuela), 103, 104, 106, 107, 116, 137
Coy, Alex, 138
Coy, Andres, Sr., 4
Coy, Andres, Jr., xi, 7, 29, 61-62, 118-119, 137
Coy, Antonio, 103, 104, 111, 137, 138, 141
Coy, Antonio de los Santos, xi
Coy, Antonio Paulino, 7
Coy, Aurelia, 137
Coy, Blas, 137
Coy, David, 137
Coy, Don Cristobal de los Santos, 1
Coy, Emmet, 7, 66, 126
Coy, Estella, 138
Coy, Ildefonso, 2, 7, 18, 19, 76, 77, 78, 104, 117, 126, 136
Coy, Ines, 137
Coy, Isabel, 137
Coy, Jacoba, 104, 105, 107, 108, 109, 112, 121, 137
Coy, Jacobo, xi, 7, 21-32, 39, 61-62, 118-119, 132, 134-135, 136, 141
Coy, Jesus, 137
Coy, Johnny, 138
Coy, Jose, 137
Coy, Jose Antonio de los Santos, 6-7
Coy, Jose Manuel, 7
Coy, Juan Jose, birth of, 6; charged with murder, 76-78, 96, 97, 98, 99, 100-102, 135, 140; children of, 39,

Index 169

49, 103-112, 137; convicted of murder, 36; as cowboy, 33-34, 58, 59, 63-64, 70, 74, 109, 112; death of, xi, 133-138, 139, 140, 147; described, xi, xii, 21, 135-136, 139; as family man, xi, 103-112, 121-124, 126, 129, 136; as friend of William Butler, 45, 58-59, 65, 69, 109-110, 116, 136; funeral for, 136; and gambling, 64-65, 113; illness of, 18, 123; indicted, 65, 140, 143; as lawman, x, xi, 34, 59, 60, 62, 71, 106, 107, 130, 135; number killed by, x, 36, 115, 139-140, 144, 147; in prison, 36-38, 97, 102, 103, 135; as railroad guard, 125-133; religion of, 115; trial of, 100-102; in Union Army, 9-12, 16, 17, 122, 123; wives of, 34, 39, 103, 104, 107, 114; wounded, 18, 34-35
Coy, Juan, Jr., 103, 106, 107, 108, 111-112, 129, 137
Coy, Juan, II, 137
Coy, Juan, III, 137
Coy, Juan (son of Victoriano and Juanita), 137
Coy, Juana Maria Luisa, 7
Coy, Juanita, 137
Coy, Manuel, 137
Coy, Manuela, 34, 39, 103, 137
Coy, Maria Antonia, 7
Coy, Maria Carmen, 7
Coy, Miguel, 141
Coy, Odel, 138
Coy, Olivia, 138
Coy, Pablino, xi, 126, 137
Coy, Refugia, 7
Coy, Rudolfo, 138
Coy, Trevinio, 77
Coy, Trinidad (daughter), 7
Coy, Trinidad, 2, 3, 6, 7, 14, 16, 39
Coy, Victor, Jr., 137
Coy, Victoria, 138
Coy, Victoriano, 103, 104, 106, 111, 129, 137
Coy City, 19, 20
Coy family, 1-5, 6-8, 16, 17, 18, 39, 54, 62, 73, 103-112
Crockett, Davy, 122
Crystal Palace, 21, 22, 24-32
Cuba, 33
Cuero, Texas, 144
Curry, Kid, xii

▪ D ▪

Dailey, C. P. "Kit," 80, 81, 86
Dailey General Merchandise Store, 88
Dailey, H. W., 146
Dailey, S. G., 80, 89, 90, 91
Dailey, Sam, 81, 90
Daileyville, 79-102, 147-148
Daileyville General Store, 80
Daileyville Riot, 36, 79-102, 135, 140
de la Garza, Rosa, 103
de la Garza, Talamantes, 103
DeWitt County, 95, 140, 143
Dodge City, Kansas, 31, 63
Dosse, John, 81
Drake, Sonny, 76, 78
Dubuis, Bishop, 60
Duval County, 13
Dyer, John, 27

▪ E ▪

Eagle Pass, 32
Edison, Thomas, 38
El Paso, Texas, 7, 144
Elder, I. L. "Fate," 76-91, 89, 91, 93, 97, 99
Elder, J. J. "Bud," 78, 83, 85, 89, 91, 93, 97, 99
Elders, 79, 91, 94
Elm Creek, 67
Escondido Creek, 8
Escondido Rifles, 8
Evans, A. Jack, 100

▪ F ▪

Falls City, 4
federalistas, 3
15th Amendment, 110
First City Bank in New York, 13
First Regiment of the Texas Cavalry (Union), 9
First State Bank of Kenedy, 146
First Texas Union Cavalry, 123
Fisher, King, 23-32, 34

Flores, Lola, 73
Floresville, 34, 64, 77, 97, 106, 107, 121, 131, 135
Floresville District Court, 92
Ford, Henry, 145
Ford, John S. "Rip," 9
Fort Sam Houston, 68
Fort Sumter, South Carolina, 8
Foster, Joe, 21, 23, 24, 27-30
Franklin, S. R., 146
Frost National Bank, 13

■ G ■

Gallagher's Saloon, 27
Garcia, Jesus, 103
Garcia, Mariano, 96
Garcia [Garza], Epitacio, 93
Garfield, James A., 38, 134
Garza, Epitacio, 36, 81, 83, 86, 89, 91, 92, 93, 94, 95, 96
Garza, Francisco, 36
Garza, Juanita, 129
Germans, 4, 69, 120, 131
Geronimo, 68, 109
Godard, Father, 103
Goliad (Karnes) County, 8
Gonzales, Texas, 79, 144
Government Hill, 109
Grand Opera House, 120
Grant, Ulysses S., 9
Graves, F. R., 83, 89, 90, 93, 100
Gray, Ada, 23-26
Green, John A., 141
Green, Robert, 141
Guenther Flour Mill, 69
Guzman brothers, 66

■ H ■

Hall, Lee, x, xi, 71, 94, 125-129
Hammack, R. L., 147
hanging tree, 60
Hankinson, T. W., 100
Hardin, John Wesley, xii, 37, 144
Harris, Jack, 21-22, 23, 27, 28, 31
Harrison, Benjamin, 109
Harrold, Eli, 80, 81, 82, 97, 100, 101
Harrold, William, 81, 82, 83, 92, 99
Hawkins, Ed, 144

Hays, Jack, xi, 6
Helena, 43, 45-57, 70, 94, 95, 121, 146
Helena Academy, 52
Helena Courthouse, 52, 56
Helena Duel, 52
Helena jail, 53
Helena Post Office, 56
Helena Union Church, 43
Hitchcock, Lieutenant, 13
Honey Ranch, 33, 62, 63, 64, 107
Houston, Sam, 8
Howard, Tom, 25-26
Huntsville, 36

■ I ■

Iles, Tom, 13
Indianola, 51, 79
Ingram, Rev. A. L., 146
Inselmann, Henry, 142
Ireland, John, 93, 94
Irish Flats, 120
Iron Front Saloon, 31

■ J ■

Jackson, Jim, 77
James, Frank, xii
James, Jesse, xii
Johnson, E. B., 123
Jones, Joseph, 123
Jordan, A. J., 97
Jourdan, Bud, 18
Journey Through Texas, xi

■ K ■

Kansas City, Missouri, 32
Karnes City, Texas, 4, 46, 54, 70, 96, 113, 118, 146
Karnes County, x, 1, 2, 8, 13, 15, 16, 19, 36, 41, 43, 45, 50, 51, 54, 70, 71, 78, 91, 94, 97, 98, 101, 131, 147
Karnes County Historical Society, 56
Karnes County National Bank, 146
Kenedy, Captain, 102
Kenedy Advance, The, 2, 146, 147
Kenedy Junction, 79, 102
Kenedy Lodge No. 774, 147

Index   171

Kenedy, Texas, 3, 46, 61, 70, 102, 121, 145
Kerrville, Texas, 144
Kimble County, 19
King Ranch, 19
King, W. H., 98
King William district, 131
Klass, Wenzel, 36
Konkele, Louis, 36
Krempkau, Albert, 129, 130-134, 139, 141-143
Krempkau, Henry, 129, 139, 141, 142
Ku Klux Klan, 68
Kusler, Henry, 142

• L •

Ladner, August, 36
Lane, E. R., 100
Laredo, ix
Las Mulas, 104
Lawhon, L. S., 100
Leal, Yldefonso, 104
Leary, Edgar, 41, 42, 44, 45, 46, 47-48, 49, 50, 95
Lee, Robert E., 9
Leonard, Theodore, 142
Leonard, Val, 142
Lincoln, Abraham, 8, 9, 38
Linder, 102
Linder, Maxine Yeater, xi, 45, 85, 99
Lipans, 7
Lodi, 64, 97
Lodi Cemetery, 136
Long Branch Saloon, 31
Longley, William, 37
Lopez, Manuel, 44
Loustannan, John, 142
Luling, 79

• M •

Mabry, Seth, 19
Manning, Joe, 44
Marquis, Lenora, 103
Martin, J. A., 147
Mason County, 19
Masonic Lodge, 56
Matamoros, Mexico, 33

Maximilian, 31
Mayfield, C. H., 100
Mayfield, Moliar, 81, 82
McCall, Sheriff, 143
McClanes, 42
McCormick, Judge, 100
McCulloch, 13
McDonald, Hugh, 44-45, 46
McDonald, Joe, 144
McNelly, L. H., 32
Mendez, Juan, 18
Menger Hotel, 108
Miller, ———, 94
Miller, T. A., 146
Mocygozemba, Mr., 5
Monroe, 64-65, 77
Morales, Pedro, 98
More, W. L., 99
Morris, T. P., 100
Museum of Natural History, 121
Mutualista, 96

• N •

Napier, Walter P., Sr., 147
Nelson, Jim, 18
New Braunfels, 1, 4, 74, 79, 131
New York, 40
New York Times, 139
Newberry, J. D., 97, 99
Newton, J. W. v. W. G. Butler, 71
Nichols, Andy, 80, 81, 82, 86, 89, 90
Nichols, J. M., 147
Nichols, J. W., 146
Niggil, Emil, 142
Noonan, George, 22
Nueces, 32
Nueces River, ix, 13
Nueces Strip, ix, 33
Nuecestown, 74
Nuevo Laredo, 96, 98

• O •

O.K. Corral, 147-148
O'Connor, Tom, 15
O'Neal, M., 102
Oakley, Annie, 40
Ochoa, Manual, 126
Oliphant, Tom, 85

Olmsted, Frederick Law, xi
Ox-Cart Road, 46, 55

▪ P ▪

Padre Island, 8
Palmito Ranch, 9
Panna Maria, 1, 4, 14, 42, 43
Panna Maria Grays, 14
Paschal, 142
Pendencia Creek, 32
Perez, Alejos, 7
Perez family, 103, 137
Perez, Jesse, xi, 21, 34, 62-67, 94, 96, 126, 127, 128-129, 134, 135
Perez, Tom, 62
Perryman, Bill, 18
Perryman, Levi, 18
Pettus, Buck, 15
Phannestein, Albert, 40
Philips, Henry, 81
Pierce, Shanghai, 32
Pine Bluff, Arkansas, 13
Pleasanton, 6, 113, 121
Polley, J. B., 100
Pony Express, 74
Potter, Ned, 51
Pullin, Henry, 86-91
Pullin, Hiram, 86-91
Pullin, Jack, 81, 86-91
Pullin, Jim, 81
Pullin, Tom, 87, 89-90
Pullin family, 93

▪ R ▪

race relations, 68-75, 111-112, 114, 120-121
railroad, 59, 70, 112, 116, 125-138, 145, 147
Reid, B. L., 101
Reupoe, John, 60
Reyes, Jacoba, 104, 137
Reyes, Juan de los, 137
Reynolds, N. G., 97
Richter, Charles, 141-142
Rio Grande, ix
Rios, Manuela, 103, 137
Rios, Mateo, 103
Ripps, Jacob, 133

Risinger, Sheriff, 41, 44, 47-48, 49
Ruckman House, 56
Ruckman, J. W., 146
Ruckman, John, 147
Ruckman, Thomas, 46, 51, 95
Rudd, L. W., 94, 96, 97
Ruppertzburg, W., 36
Rutledge, John, 97
Rutledge, W. J., 147

▪ S ▪

Saila, Cleta, 103
San Antonio and Aransas Pass Railroad, 54, 70, 136, 137, 129
San Antonio Archdiocese, 103
San Antonio Daily Express, 43, 50, 91, 93, 94, 95, 96, 97, 98, 100, 136, 139, 140, 141, 144
San Antonio Daily Herald, 3, 34, 36, 39, 40
San Antonio Daily Light, 70, 73, 77, 139
San Antonio Evening Express, 30
San Antonio Police Department, 144
San Antonio River, 46, 69, 108
San Antonio, Texas, xi, xii, 1, 2, 22, 24-32, 39-40, 61, 68, 72, 79, 95, 107-109, 113, 114, 120-124, 128
San Diego, Texas, 13
San Fernando Cathedral, 108
San Fernando de Bexar, 1
San Francisco, California, 7
San Francisco de los Tejas, 1
San Jacinto, Battle of, 2
San Pedro Park, 122
Sanchez, Cebelo, 90
Sanchez, Dario, 96
Sanders, Bill, 63, 65
Sandoval, Antonio, 134
Santa Anna, Antonio Lopez de, 2
Santleman, August, 142
Sarran, Ed, 132, 133, 135
Schoenart, Anton, 36
Scott County, Mississippi, 86
Scott, Lieutenant, 45, 50
Seale, Rev. E. Y., 104
Second Texas Cavalry, 9

Index 173

Seffel, Frank, 36
Seguin, Texas, 111, 144
Selman, John, 144
Sheero, 135
Shuler, John, 81, 82
Silesian Poles, 4-5, 43
Simms, Billy, 22, 27
Singer family, 8
Sioux Indians, 116
Six-Shooter Junction, 102
62nd U.S. Colored Infantry, 9
slavery, 8, 75
Smith, A. V., 101
Smith, George H., 96
Southern Hotel, 126
Spechts, 131
Spooner, T. H., 100
Sporting District, xii, 25, 27, 72-73, 108, 124
St. Louis, 63
Star, The, 119
State Capitol, 19
states' rights, 8
Stevenson, A. R., 100
Sullivan, John L., 18, 83
Sumpter County, Alabama, 60

• T •

Taylor, Alf, 81
Taylor-Sutton Feud, 71, 98
Teas, W. A., 146
Teel, T. T., 100
Texas Cavalry, 10-11
Texas Department of Criminal Justice, 34, 36
Texas Rangers, x, xi, 6-7, 32, 37, 45, 71, 93, 94, 98, 126-127
37th District Court, 141, 142
Thompson, Ben, 21-32, 95
Thompson, Mary Anne, 22
Tombstone, Arizona, 147
Tovar, 35
Trader, Dr., 95
Travieso, Jacoba, 104
Travieso, Tomas, 137
Travis, William B., 122

Trent, Florence, 73
Trevino, 140, 143
Trimble, John, 80, 85, 92
True West, 43
Turner Hall Opera House, 24, 25, 107
Twohig, John, 2-4

• U •

Union Pacific, 37
Uvalde, 23, 31, 32, 70

• V •

Vara, Maria del Refugio, 7
Victoria Advocate, 94
Von Ormy, Texas, x

• W •

Waco, Texas, 127
Wagner, 137
Walton, D. A. T., 147
Webb County Jail, 96
Wild West Show, 40
Wiatrek, 110
Wilkes, Franklin C., 8
Williams, Melissa, 144
Wilson County, 1, 34, 36, 65, 78, 95, 97, 100, 104, 130, 137, 140, 143
Wilson County Courthouse, 36
Wilson, James, 100
"Wofford Crossing Road," xi, 45, 85, 102
Wood, Charley, 81
Wounded Knee, 116

• X–Y •

Ximenes, Sheriff, 34, 65
XIT, 19
Yoakum, Benjamin Franklin, 46
Yoakum, Mr., xii
Yoakum, Texas, 70, 127, 129
Young, Bill, 76, 77
Young, William, 117

About the Authors

CHARLES L. OLMSTED, a native of Lake Charles, Louisiana, has written for the *Lake Charles* (La.) *American Press,* the *Helotes* (Texas) *Echo,* the *San Antonio Express-News,* the *San Antonio Light,* and the *Metrocom* (Universal City, Texas) *Herald.* He has won writing awards from the Louisiana Sports Writers Association and the Texas Community Newspaper Association, Inc. and publication awards from the NAIA-Sports Information Directors Association.

EDWARD COY YBARRA, a native of San Antonio, is president of Munguia Printers, Inc., a family-owned company that has been serving the printing needs of San Antonio since 1934. He has been active in the community through his participation in various organizations, and currently serves as a board member of the San Antonio Police Youth Education, a drug and gang prevention organization.

www.ingramcontent.com/pod-product-compliance
Lightning Source LLC
Chambersburg PA
CBHW061310110426
42742CB00012BA/2130